THE NUMB

# LEARNING
# MASONIC
# RITUAL

## THE SIMPLE,
## SYSTEMATIC AND
## SUCCESSFUL WAY TO
## MASTER THE WORK

### Rick Smith

English Craft Masonic Constitution Edition

RICK SMITH

Also Available on Amazon Kindle

From the Same Author:
"Learning Royal Arch Chapter Ritual"

# CONTENTS

For My Mentors – You Know Who You Are

# PREFACE

## The Secret Weapons of Great Ritualists Revealed for Everyone to Use

Dozens of books have been written about Learning Masonic Ritual, so what makes this one different?

If you are new to Freemasonry and facing Ritual for the first time, or alternately you have tried and struggled with Ritual in the past, it might be helpful to have a system to follow that will boost your chances of success.

Over the past twenty years I have had hundreds of conversations with other Freemasons about Learning Masonic Ritual. Based on those discussions, and my own experiences, I have identified the Secret Weapons of Successful Ritualists, and combined them into a working system that anyone can use to succeed.

Many people struggle with Masonic Ritual because they simply don't have a reliable system for learning it.

How do great Masonic Ritualists make it look so easy? In this book, you will learn their techniques and processes, and how to apply them for yourself.

As you follow this step-by-step system, you will learn;

- How to get offered the Work you want

- How to set up a Working Timetable so you peak at the right time

- The 3 Stage Plan that will keep you on-track

- Memorisation Tricks and Techniques

- How to find Rehearsal Time when there is none

- How to become a great Worshipful Master

You will also be able to avoid the big mistakes which people often make;

- They don't allow Enough Time

- They don't have a System, so they do it the hard way

- They fail to get the Hard Work done early, so they're always playing catch-up

- They don't utilise the Learning Aids that are littered throughout the Ritual

- They don't know how to Overcome Nerves and Gain Confidence

One of the most effective ways to advance your Masonic Enlightenment is to actively immerse yourself in becoming a competent Ritual performer in your Lodge. There are many techniques you could employ, most of them very simple, and they are collected here for you to try. In places, I have also drawn on my experience as a veteran communications professional and as a certified Clinical Hypnotherapist.

If you are starting out in the Craft and looking for guidance in the Ritual system, or maybe you tried to learn Ritual but struggled with the performance aspects, this book is for you.

# HOW TO USE THIS BOOK

Learning is challenging. It isn't technically difficult in itself, but it takes time and patience to do it properly. As you go on you find different methods that work better, and you eliminate the more time-consuming and less productive ones. You are evolving.

Given enough time, you might eventually arrive at the perfect formula, but it could take years of trial and error.

If you follow the System in this book, you will learn the most effective methods now, and you can immediately put them into practice.

### Three Steps You Can Take

The first step in becoming a competent Ritualist is to commit to the process, to actually want to succeed.

The second step is to understand that, though it will look like a mountain ahead of you in the beginning, you have no reason to doubt your ability to climb it. Thousands have been there before you, and succeeded.

The third step is to take it head-on, using every tool and resource you can find, and master it.

That's the way I did it, and over twenty years I was able to test and trial different techniques until I found I had a great system that works. I didn't invent this plan, it's the way that excellent Ritualists develop their skills and techniques, the ones they continue to use for many years, to 'make it look easy'.

### A New Approach?

Time is the most important factor. Let's assume that you are motivated to succeed, but you also have a real life! If this is going to work for you, it can't be disruptive. So, no long boring periods of study and no disruption to your daily routine.

You need a System.

Step-by-step you will learn a successful approach to memorising the Work and practicing the delivery, ready for your big day in the Lodge. If you follow this systematic approach, trying all the elements until you find the personal combination that works for you, you will greatly improve your knowledge and capabilities for delivering strong Ritual performances in your Lodge.

The key elements of this process are;

- Measuring the Work: understanding how much time you will need and planning your timetable.

- Memorising the Ritual: Front-end loading the process by diving in and quickly committing the key passages to memory

- Polishing the Work: The right (and wrong) ways to really get to grips with your Ritual and eliminate all the obstacles to a great performance.

- Rehearsal, Preparation and Delivery: How it will be for you on the day

You can use this book in two ways;

You can read it from cover to cover, and get comfortable with the whole system before you try it out. You will understand the beginning, the middle, and the end, and you can pick out any areas which particularly apply to you. In this case, the book should be followed in Chapter sequence.

Alternately, you may just jump straight to the parts that you need, but in this case, please make sure you read Chapter 3, which outlines the Three-Stage System which you should be following.

## Additional Resources

You can register for regular updates on www.learningmasonicritual.com and leave questions and comments in the Community section. Ask for help on specific Ritual, and someone is bound to have tips and tricks to add to your armoury.

Please 'Like' our Facebook Page 'Learning Masonic Ritual' and join in the discussions.

If you find something in this book which helps you, and I truly hope you will, please post an appropriate review on Amazon and give the book a star rating! Make your contribution to raising Ritual standards in our Lodges, and ensuring the popularity and relevance of Freemasonry in the future.

Thank You

Rick Smith

12th June 2013

London, England

rs@learningmasonicritual.com

RICK SMITH

# 1
# SO, WHAT IS RITUAL?

So, you're a Freemason, eh? Feels good, doesn't it!

At least it will once you get through the first few years, and you begin to piece together what's going on during the Ceremonies. You'll be fine! All that quaint language the Brethren spout during the Ceremonies? That's all going to magically fall into place, of course it is! Before you know it you're going to be reeling off Degree Ceremonies from the Master's Chair, or maybe Tracing Board Lectures from the floor. Address to the Brethren? Piece of cake! Charge After Passing? Bring it on, why don't you!

Except it probably isn't going to be that simple for most of us.

There are many remarkable human beings who can effortlessly memorise and regurgitate long passages of awkward English prose. They are, however, in the minority. Plus, an even smaller minority are those who can not only remember the Work, but also deliver it with style and character so that it's interesting for the audience and particularly for the Candidate.

Most Masonic Ritual is directed at a Candidate who is usually hearing it for the first time, and who will make a judgment about his engagement with Freemasonry based in part on how he engages with the Ritual being directed his way.

So, here are the two basic rules of good Ritual;

1. You need to know your stuff.

2. You cannot be boring.

Lucky for you that you have this Book to guide you!

## THE PURPOSE OF THE RITUAL

Traditionally, the primary purpose of the Ritual is to *educate* the Candidate. This is a big part of the grand design of Masonry. But it's a huge challenge too.

### How Receptive Is The Candidate Likely To Be?

In reality, when a Candidate offers himself for Initiation he's usually quite nervous. Of course (and we've all said this to a trembling initiate at one time or another) every Brother starts from the same position. Later in our Masonic careers we come to understand the purposes and procedures of the Ceremonies. Sitting on the backbenches, or from the safety of a Principal Officer's chair, we have time to observe and absorb the Ritual when it's being performed by someone else. There isn't any pressure on us.

But for the Candidate it's entirely different!

Unless he's been illicitly briefed in advance, a new Initiate has very little idea about what is happening. He is relying mainly on sound and touch to interpret what is going on around him. It's hard to believe, no matter how well the Ritual Ceremony is delivered, that the poor guy is actually in a position to learn anything at all! But he is having an educational experience nonetheless.

What is actually imparted is an initial impression of

Freemasonry, a powerful lesson in humility, reliance, and ultimately, Brotherhood.

In the Second Degree the pressure is marginally less, but even then the Candidate is being taken into an unknown situation, which is still not an ideal environment for learning.

Then comes the Third Degree, quite unlike anything else!

The Candidate's overall *experience* during the ceremonies is the education that sticks.

## It's All About A Smooth Meeting

Whilst it may be true that the original purpose of the Ritual is to educate the Candidate, in reality it is the wholeness of the Ceremony that will be remembered by most everyone in the Lodge. The smoothness, consistency and demeanour with which it is conducted, the accuracy and conformity to the 'Book', and the pleasure and satisfaction which result from good Teamwork will matter far more to the Brethren. It simply makes for a better meeting.

We've established that the Candidate's impressions will be derived from the firm and secure way that he is handled by the Working Deacon. In practical terms, this is more important than any minor success he may have in deciphering the language and absorbing the lessons!

He will have plenty of time to observe the Ceremonies in the future, once he's made a Master Mason. For the purpose of performing the Ceremonies, what's most important is that the Working Officers achieve the competence and confidence to execute a satisfactory Ceremony for the benefit of everyone present in the Temple.

## Channeling Your Inner Actor!

Other authors on the subject urge the reader to channel their "inner-actor". This is wise advice; however it is unlikely to work for everyone. Masons are drawn from every walk of life and most people can't really *act* in a convincing way. There are some truly amazing Ritualists, who deliver Ritual almost as a piece of entertainment. I have to admit great admiration towards these Brethren, but there aren't so many of them out there in the Craft.

Maybe Ritual is more like a Business Presentation than a theatrical performance? When you stand up in the Lodge, you are setting out to demonstrate your expertise in a particular subject (the Ritual), whilst holding the audience's attention. In business, the stakes are often high, so the pressure to perform is real. Many more of us will experience this real-life business situation than will ever give a theatrical performance.

Great Ritual is all about striking a balance between your own competence and capabilities, and the environment in which you are called upon to "perform". It might be described as a cross between 'camouflage' and 'context'.

Later we will discuss various techniques such as metering, intonation, rhythm and posture which go together to achieve a balanced delivery. What matters most, once the techniques are in place, is *sincerity*. This is a natural way to deliver the Ceremony, but of course it requires empathy and understanding of the Ritual that you're doing. As you will learn later, this is not difficult to acquire.

### Shoulders Back, Chest Out...

Only around one third of everyday communication is purely verbal. Broad-channel communication, as any public speaker or presenter knows, is only achieved visually and emotionally when the body language is right.

Some writers have gone to great lengths and describe in some detail the posture that you should adopt whilst delivering (for example) a Charge or a Tracing Board Lecture. Although it may be great to be able to puff up your chest, hold total eye contact, and control the movement of your hands in concert with the delivery of the vocal element, this mastery will take time to develop.

In your early days, you just need to find your own comfort zone as regards posture, movement, and gesticulation. As a Ritualist, you will benefit a great deal if you can 'centre' yourself.

When you are delivering a two-thousand word monologue in front of knowledgeable and critical audience, you'll have enough to think about without having to worry about how you look. So you will find later in the book that we'll focus more on relaxation as a means of achieving confidence and competent delivery, rather than precise positioning. There are tricks and tips which will enable you to convert nervousness and stress into excitement and enthusiasm.

## How Ritual Works

If you are new to the Craft, typical Craft Ritual workings, dominated in England by Emulation and Taylors, with many variants such as West End, Logic, D.M Goudielock etc., revolve around the period during which the First Temple at Jerusalem was built by King Solomon. The stories build from a peaceful and regal beginning which explains the inspiration for and construction of the Temple, leading up to a cataclysmic event which has come to symbolise the central morality of Speculative Freemasonry. Throughout this series of short 'plays', you'll come across dozens of metaphors, imparting the moral criteria which a Freemason is expected to aspire to.

The Ritual is composed of exquisitely crafted language, and for most Masons the messages go in and stay in, enabling them to live more positive and fulfilled lives.

## Masonry and Religion

It's hard to avoid the perception of parts of the outside world that there are quasi-religious elements to Masonry. I have met some great guys who have purposely avoided Masonry because they feel that it would be 'too religious' for them.

If you have no issues with attending a church wedding or funeral, or being a Godfather for someone's new baby, you should not meet any greater religious demands in Craft Freemasonry. Masonry and its members respect religion, and are completely at ease with each other's beliefs, whatever they may be. Masons do not worship in Craft Lodges; that is the role of the Church.

Beyond the Three Degrees, there are numerous other Masonic Orders, many of which welcome those of a more serious religious inclination, such as the Rose Croix and the Knights Templars. That's your private business in the future.

The obvious overlap between Religion and Freemasonry is Morality, which both teach as their primary function. The key difference in their approach is that fundamental religion tends towards 'God-Fearing Morality' whilst Craft Masonry speaks more to the Moral Compass, and the idea that your behaviour in life should be geared towards preserving the stability of society and the happiness of everyone around you.

It appears that the historical basis for English Craft Ritual is largely grounded in the Old Testament of the King James Bible. If you are interested in exploring this aspect of Masonic origin further, there is an excellent book on the subject by Mike Neville, called "Sacred Secrets, Freemasonry, The Bible, and Christian Faith" which explains all the links throughout Craft Masonry and many of the other Allied Orders.

For the purpose of learning and executing Masonic Craft Ritual, religion has no direct relevance whatsoever.

## What Are You Seeking?

Freemasonry is all about 'pulling in the same direction' If we frame Ritual in that context, the Ritualists role is to fit smoothly into the overall environment of the Lodge, and to dovetail with the other Officers and Brethren in achieving a seamless progression through the meeting. People will remember when things go right, people will remember when things go wrong, but people, particularly Masons, are disconcerted by large swings between the positive and the negative during the course of the Lodge proceedings.

What this Book and it's methodology attempts to do, therefore, is to give the aspiring Ritualist a practical and pragmatic approach to the methods and skills needed to perform Ritual to an acceptable standard in the Lodge. It is taken as a given fact that you are a Freemason 'In Your Heart' and so it stays away from the moral aspects of the Craft.

And remember, everyone wants you to succeed!

## So Why Do You Want To 'Do' Ritual?

We all meet great Ritualists during our Masonic Careers. Guys who make it look so easy, rattling off Tracing Boards and Mystical Lectures with one hand symbolically tied behind their back. To them, it seems so effortless, and to some of us, so daunting. Often, the common reaction is to defeat yourself before you even get started. You classify yourself as a 'non-Ritualist'.

That's a shame, because it really isn't so difficult if you have a system to follow.

If you're serious about participating in your Lodge's proceedings, you may decide to aim for a 'non-Ritual' role, and specialize in it, such as Treasurer, Almoner, or Charity Steward. All these are noble callings, and essential to the smooth running of the Lodge. Each also demands an amount of oratory, so you'll have a strong presence in the Lodge meeting, as you give your regular reports. And your work will be greatly appreciated.

The problem with this strategy is that you will probably have to go through the Chair before you will be considered for any of these Offices. That will mean that you'll need to perform substantial amounts of the Ritual in the Book.

There are also some practical considerations along the way.

Though many Lodges are over-subscribed and never short of Officers, there are many others, one of which you may be a member of, who either have just enough Candidates coming through to maintain a complete progression for the Offices, or worse, have too few Candidates and are forced to refill Offices with Past Masters on a regular basis. In these Lodges, there is sometimes justification for Candidates to leap-frog Offices because of expediency.

Whatever the case, it's a long game. If your Lodge has a healthy attitude to bringing Candidates through the Offices and the associated Ritual and Ceremonies, you will have many great years and many opportunities to participate in the Work. It won't all happen at once, although sometimes it might feel that way.

Even the smallest piece of well-delivered Ritual gives great satisfaction. A competent Inner Guard, who gets the words right and is always on time with his perambulations and salutes is great to watch. Good interplay between the Inner Guard and the Junior Warden, and directly to the Master in some Ceremonies, is one of the key foundations of a successful meeting.

So, if you've read this far you should now have a warm feeling about the value of Ritual to yourself and the Lodge, and hopefully some positive interest in learning the skills to take part.

## RITUAL REWARDS

Once you have that warm feeling, it's only reasonable to look at the rewards that come with mastering the Work.

### Your Masonic Legacy

Whenever anyone in my Lodge mentions a Brother who has passed, they often tag him with "He was a Great Ritualist". It is remembered, as it is a little part of your legacy! If you join Masonry in mid-life, you will form multiple friendships that could endure for twenty or thirty years, which is a long time! These relationships matter in your life. You should aim to be respected in as many of your walks of life as possible, and Ritual is no different.

### Competition For Offices

By involving yourself enthusiastically in the work, you will raise your profile in the Lodge and you could improve your chances of being chosen for Office. This is important in Lodges where there is competition for offices. Most important is LoI, because that's where you can get yourself noticed for effort and results. We'll cover that in more detail later.

### Where Is It All Leading?

One day you will hopefully arrive at the Chair, and your year as Master will largely be remembered for the way you conduct the Lodge Business. The perfect Master's Year scenario is that you have enough Candidates in the pipeline that you get the chance to do all three Degree Ceremonies. To guarantee this, it's a really great idea to line yourself up a Candidate of your own for your Masters Year!

When you are the Master it's your prerogative, under advisement from the Secretary and the Lodge Standing Committee, to allocate the Work for each meeting. This is second only in importance to choosing the menu for the Festive Board!

It's actually up to you to decide how much of the years' Work is in your own hands.

I come across Masters over the years that had great intentions on their way to the Chair, but when they got there it all went a bit pear-shaped! People's circumstances change, and sometimes family or professional factors impact on the Master's spare time, leaving him overloaded and simply too busy to commit to the full Ritual load. However, sometimes he simply underestimated the upswing in work that comes with the Chair.

This is one of the most important things that you need to know before you take the Master's Oath.

Finding themselves over-stretched, Masters often welcome the opportunity to farm-out some of the Ceremonies. If this results in them missing the chance to perform the Degree Ceremonies during their year, that's a shame. Because once you are through the Chair and out the other side, it's hard to get invited back 'in' for a Ceremony that no-one ever saw you perform, and you might not get back in the Chair as Master again for many years, if ever.

So, the message is this; everything that you learn and do in the Lodge is leading up to your Masters Year, and there is only one right way to approach that; All The Way In.

### Rewards For The Inner Man

They say that "Politics is Showbiz for Ugly People". For the rest of us there's Masonry!

Ritual's primary purpose is to implant the moral metaphors of Masonic teaching. That's unequivocal. Put it aside.

For our purposes, we're concentrating on two main factors;

Firstly, how your Ritual performance will enhance the well-being of the Lodge, and secondly, how it makes you feel. When you do your Work, you should get a sense of achievement each time you take on something challenging and deliver it well.

## Engagement, Understanding, and Enjoyment – The Virtuous Circle

You will develop a greater understanding of the meaning of Craft Masonry, and will experience a more inclusive experience at Lodge meetings. You'll be 'part of the action' which is a lot more interesting and stimulating than simply observing from the side-lines. Almoners Reports, Charity Stewards Reports, Treasurers Reports, the Risings and so on, whilst a necessary and integral part of the Lodge Business, can be awfully tedious if that's all you do at the meeting.

Many people don't get involved because they lack confidence. It's understandable. Everyone gets nervous, but some people just accept it as a limitation and never get to experience the thrill and stimulus of performance. If you feel overwhelmed and nervous, all I ask is that you first accept that there might be a way through it for you, so that you can join in too.

## Enhancing Your Communication Skills

If you put in the effort, which is a positive experience once you commit to it, your public communication skills, particularly in business, will be significantly enhanced by your new confidence in front of an audience. I have been giving board-room presentations for thirty years now, and I can honestly say that I became really good at it once I had gained the extra confidence and delivery skills by doing a few Tracing Boards and Charges in the Lodge.

## The Toolbox Of Techniques

Provided you commit a little time to the process, you can access the toolbox of techniques. Most people have the basic intellectual ability to do quite complex things, but some fall short because they lack the system and guidance to apply their resources in a structured way.

Some mistakenly believe that if you read something enough times it will magically enter your brain, lodge there, and simply deliver itself on demand, perfectly. This is the "It'll be all right on the night" school of Masonic Ritual. It rarely works.

Others are in possession of the basic tools and techniques, and may indeed be quite eloquent once they are on their feet in the Lodge, but invariably simply do not allow themselves enough time in the run-up to the meeting. Of course it is possible to 'learn' a short piece such as the Charge to the Initiate in a matter of a few days, but when it comes to the delivery you will be working from short-term memory alone, and this introduces a significant performance risk. Learning Ritual is not just about being able to memorise things.

So, I hope that this preamble has got you thinking, and perhaps it's stimulated your curiosity to go a little bit further.

### The Line Of Commitment

In Sports Psychology, a powerful branch of Hypnosis and NLP, one popular technique is called the "Line of Commitment". It's an imaginary line on the ground which you visualise before you step over it to take your shot, kick the ball, serve at tennis, or whatever is your sporting trigger. I'll explain it more later, but here is your first Line of Commitment.

Right here is where you decide to commit to following these systems and processes to improve your chances of becoming a competent Ritualist in your Lodge.

Just think it through for a moment. Imagine how it's going to be for you the first time you stand up in the Lodge and deliver a great performance for the Candidate, for your Brethren, and for Yourself.

When you're ready, step over the Line of Commitment

## 2
# THE CHALLENGES OF RITUAL

**Some People Make It Look So Easy!**

The truth is that there's really not much to it, in Craft Ritual. You learn it, you deliver it, everyone pats you on the back, and you move on. So why do so many apparently capable people find it so terribly daunting?

There are plenty of Masons who have acquired or developed the skills to manage Ritual without too many obstacles. Some people appear naturally talented at this. In truth they'll tell you that it's a lot of hard work to achieve a good standard, but they have systems and processes that work for them.

If you've struggled with Ritual in the past, you probably fall into one of two categories;

- You don't have a reliable system for learning, and/or

- You struggle with your confidence.

## THE SECRETS OF GREAT RITUALISTS

### Allowing Enough Time

The first and most important reason why people fail is because they don't allow nearly enough time.

People tend to think in terms of weeks, whereas most people should really be thinking in terms of months. This the main reason why people struggle to cross the finishing line in time for the meeting. It is the most important factor.

The objective of good time-planning is to get yourself to a peak of competence exactly when you need to be there, on the day of the Meeting. This needs a long-view, and an honest reality-check at the start. Learning Ritual is not really an art, it's more like a science. It cries out for process. If you make a reasonably accurate timetable and stick to the process, you will succeed.

### Different Kinds of Time

Some people think that they can pick up the Book the night before and that by reading it through a few times, it will magically stick.

It doesn't work.

Even if you appreciate that much more time is required, not all time is created equal. You might think, for instance, that it will typically take twenty hours to learn a particular ceremony to a competent standard. You might therefore conclude that three hours a day for the week before the meeting will have you right there on the day.

This would be a mistake because nobody can possibly focus on a single task for three hours every day! But the second dimension is this; learning is a distillation process. Active concentration on the task is only part of the process. To learn effectively, to 'distil' something properly, there's a lot going on in the background.

So the same twenty hours, consumed at a slower rate, will be much more effective. Twenty minutes a day, spread over two months, is a much more reliable method. Twenty minutes of active study is likely to result in many times that in passive learning (cooking) which will take place in your subconscious without any noticeable effort.

## Good Learning Technique

To repeat, Time is the most important ingredient of learning and delivering good Ritual. If you were to stop reading this book right now (please don't) you have already learned the most important lesson.

The second reason why people fall short is because they employ ineffective learning techniques.

## Audio Recording?

There's one technique which most Masons try at some time, because it's such a blatantly obvious short-cut, and that's Audio Recording.

I would be a hypocrite if I said that Audio Recording has no place in this process. I sometimes use it to check myself against a written copy. It's an easy way to spot where you are habitually going wrong. Its application in the rehearsal stage might be useful for some people, copyright notwithstanding!

However, the idea that repeatedly listening to a recording of a Ceremony is going to magically work for you is probably a blind alley. Experience suggests that this method tends to fail when the pressure is on. Relying only on your auditory sense to implant the sequences and language of the Ritual in your mind, and enable them for recall, is a risky business.

There's another thing about Audio Recording, which I've heard from quite a number of Masons. It's sort of Taboo.

One common interpretation of the 'Secrets' is that they are words that are never written out longhand, especially in the Ritual book. The rest of the Ritual is just written language which is available to anyone, so if you re-write part of it to make it more portable, such as a smartphone or Kindle, although you must pay due respect to any copyright issues, you shouldn't breach any of your Obligations of Secrecy.

But there's something about Audio Recording that sometimes makes it feel like cheating. That's why I usually don't include it in my learning system.

### Get Lost… In The Language

It's useful to immerse yourself in the Ritual passage you are trying to learn. Masonic 'language' is peppered with patterns, alliteration and links which can be smartly harnessed to aid the important memory recall process which is part of the performance package you're now following.

Taken as a whole, something like an Obligation, Charge, or Tracing Board Lecture looks daunting, and it's certainly a challenge to learn any of these for the first time. But you can be sure that this Work is packed full of imagery, memory cues, patterns and clues to help you learn it and deliver it well. Some people never discover these aids because they simply view the passage as a succession of words and sentences.

In this sense I'm talking only about the language used, not the meaning of the story. 'Understanding' the Ritual is a big subject all of its own, which is covered more fully later in the book.

### Bite Sized Pieces

Another set of attributes which are 'designed-in' to the Ritual are natural break points. As a quick demonstration of this, try the following exercise;

1. On your PC's word processor, type in the Ritual passage you are learning now. If it's a really long one, just do a couple of pages. Make sure you type in the punctuation accurately.

2. Next, use the Return key to break the passage down into mini-paragraphs of no more than three sentences (only one or two if they're long ones).

3. Now use the numbering tool to automatically number each paragraph.

4. Those numbers will tell you the number of days you will need to commit the words to memory, following the system you'll learn in this book.

Breaking the whole into easy parts will speed up the learning process and give you clear milestones to measure your progress. It may seem obvious to you, but you'd be surprised how many people don't do it this way.

This simple exercise should have immediately introduced the idea of a systematic approach to learning your work. We'll develop the techniques shortly, and you'll start to see the benefits immediately.

## Anatomy of the Ritualist

An identifying characteristic of most decent Ritualists is Confidence. Many people are capable of learning complex and demanding passages from the Ritual Book, but hold themselves back because they lack the confidence to deliver the end-result. Having this obstacle in the road ahead, no matter how distant, induces self-defeat right at the outset. Simply put; "I won't be able to do this on the day, so what's the point in trying to learn it?"

The Ritualist has probably been there, but got past it. So will you, if you follow the system and believe in your ability to do things you've never tried before, if you're shown the right techniques. It's called Learning, but it's just as much about Growing.

You'll generally have a minimum of seven or eight years from Initiation to Installation, and that presents you with lots of opportunities to learn, practice, and prepare to be the Ritualist that lurks inside all of us!

## Your First Ritual Has Already Happened!

Your first encounter with Masonic Ritual was the Questions in the Second and Third Degree Ceremonies. Guess what; whilst you were progressing through your own Three Degrees, you were already being introduced to the Ritual process by being asked to learn the answers to those important questions that the Master asked you.

In the popular Craft workings, such as Taylors and Emulation, these Questions are standard, and the Candidate should always have a Deacon alongside him to prompt his answers.

It's not unheard of for Candidates to answer faultlessly, and many do. Those that do have put in the work to learn the answers. Those that don't have not; it really is that simple. My experience is that a Candidate who's Proposer has clearly explained what's expected of him will learn and answer well. A Candidate who has not had the oral implications of Masonry fully explained may not realize that this is part of a test, and one worth passing.

Because learning and confidently delivering the answers to those Questions could be your first step to becoming a Ritualist!

## Don't Expect Instant Enlightenment!

Once you become a Master Mason, you will be given your first Ritual Book (hereinafter, the 'Book'). You might take it home and put it in a drawer and come back to it years later, which would be a shame. You might try to read it, and realize, like most things in the early stage of your Masonic journey, it doesn't mean much to you, especially since a lot of the words are blanked out or abbreviated.

Don't worry! Nobody 'gets it' first time. It *is* confusing, it's *meant* to be that way.

Over time it will start to form structures and patterns which will develop your understanding of what's going on behind the scenes. Masonry is just a big collection of metaphors for life, and the Ceremonies and Rituals contained in the little Book are just stories, acted out in the Lodge to provide a delivery mechanism for the messages of morality to be conveyed and implanted.

At first, the Book can seem like Double-Dutch. And even when you first encounter some of the Ritual Ceremonies in the Lodge, they may not make much sense to you either. It takes time to form itself into a structure; the Third Degree Ceremony talks about 'the connection of our whole system and the relative dependence of its several parts' and eventually things will become clearer.

But you can do better. By attacking every opportunity to learn and deliver Ritual, you will begin to understand how it all fits together, and that will really enhance your enjoyment of being in the Lodge.

## THE BASICS

Here's an explanation of how the Offices progress, the particular skill sets that you need for each one, and the variances between them. If you're already heading for the Chair and you know all this stuff, please feel free to skip to the next section.

### The Offices and How They Work

The order of succession through the Offices goes something like this;

*Steward;* No walking and no talking. Lots of Obedience and Submission.

*Inner Guard;* Lots of short walks and a few words, but very visible.

*Junior Deacon;* Lots of walking and quite a lot of talking. The JD's work on an Initiation is the first really big challenge of your progression through the Offices. This book will teach you how to memorise the perambulations as well as the language.

*Senior Deacon;* Lots of walking and some talking. It's more complicated than JD, but you are a year further on in experience so it's probably about the same task load.

*The Wardens;* Now you stop walking! The Junior and Senior Wardens only really move around during the Raising Ceremony. But you must learn how to close the Third Degree properly.

*The Worshipful Master;* He stands up and sits down a lot, and does a great deal of gavelling. He only gets to move in the Third Degree Ceremony. An immense amount of talking!

So, there's a clear evolution from walking to not-walking. Conversely, you evolve from silence to conducting most or all the Ceremonies yourself, in the space of seven Offices. In many Lodges that means its seven years from Initiation to the Chair. That sounds like a long time, but if you only meet four times a year that's about one month of afternoons and three-course suppers! Luckily it's spread out over time, and in Ritual terms it's really the time *between* the meetings that's most important.

So now you are armed with all this motivation, let's get on with the Plan.

3

# MAKE YOUR PLAN

In this Chapter, we're going to 'Measure the Work'. That means estimating the task ahead and setting up a schedule to ensure you achieve your aims.

The first time you learn a new piece of work it will be challenging and it will take time. However, a well-considered and well-constructed plan will carry most of your load, provided you stick to it.

Obviously the more time you can allow yourself, the better you will do. But if you do it properly, the next time you come back to do it again it will be much simpler to revise and polish. In fact, you will probably become very good at this. If you follow the right systems, you could even be on your way to becoming a 'specialist' in some areas of the Ritual.

## Go and Watch a Ceremony Before You Learn It

When you are sitting in a Lodge, and you watch a major Ceremony being performed, it's quite hard to fathom how that complex piece of Masonic theatre could possibly be condensed into twenty or thirty pages of that tiny Book in your pocket.

The truth is it isn't!

In 'conventional' English Craft Masonry, the Book is really just a guide to the protocol and language. It's really not practical to try to learn a whole Ceremony, particularly one which involves multiple participants and perambulations, simply by using the Book as a script. Ritual is so much more than that.

In this respect, the Lodge of Instruction is invaluable. However as a starting point for your first Ceremony, there's no substitute for seeing a live 'performance'.

For example; If you have never seen an Initiation Ceremony you must arrange to see at least one or two whilst you're learning the JD's work. The same goes for the Senior Deacon with the Passing and Raising Ceremonies. You should arrange to see this as soon as you can, so that you get a clear picture of the floor-work. Nobody will mind if you make notes on the back of your summons, or sketch a drawing, but it will really help to give the Ritual some context once you dive into the Book.

I have checked. There are no training videos on YouTube!

**Visiting Other Lodges**

Visiting is often called the 'Life Blood of Freemasonry', and some of the members of your Lodge will be regular visitors to other Lodges. Ask around, and it's almost certain that someone will be overjoyed to take you along to another Lodge where you can see what you need to see.

Most Lodges welcome visitors. Just ask the Secretary of your Lodge to suggest one or two friendly Lodges that you could contact, and e-mail their Secretaries. Or ask your Lodge Tyler, who will know which work that each of his Lodges is doing in the coming weeks. But please try to find a way to see the Ceremony you are learning early on. It will make a huge difference to your initial progress to put the whole thing into context at the beginning.

On no account should you be shy about visiting. If you visit the same Lodge often enough, you may eventually become a PIG (Permanently Invited Guest).

## THE SYSTEM

In the first chapter you found out that a key reason why people struggle with Ritual is that they don't have a structured process to follow, including allowing the right amount of time. In this section, we'll explore a System to take care of this.

We're focusing on Three Stages in a Process, which, when correctly followed, will ensure you reach your optimum performance standard just before your 'Target Meeting'.

The Three Stages are these;

### Stage One: Cramming

In this stage, you are going to focus on memorizing your part of the Work as quickly as possible, to 85% - 90% accuracy. The objective of Stage One is to get to a position where you can recite the Work all the way through, without stopping, even if it is a little inaccurate. The idea is that you will quickly acquire enough knowledge to be able to understand the language and the flow of the Ceremony, which will give you a solid launch-pad from which to propel yourself through the next two stages.

### Stage Two: Polishing

In this stage, you are going to take the Work you have memorised in Stage One, and start to correct your errors, using some techniques which you will learn shortly, whilst the Ceremony embeds itself in your long term memory. You will be using some of your subconscious abilities to really 'learn' the Work, so that you can then begin to concentrate on the Performance and Delivery aspects.

## Stage Three: Rehearsal

In this stage, you will have memorised and learned both the Work and the meanings behind it, and now you will start to focus on 'performing' it, which will enable you to discover many of the inbuilt rhythms and patterns in the Ceremony. By tieing all these methods together, you will gain both confidence and competence. You can expect to arrive at a point where you are in possession of all the attributes to deliver an excellent performance in the Meeting.

In order to allocate these three Stages correctly, we first need to look at the Time-Line.

## PLANNING THE WORK

There are two distinctly different types of Ritual, which require slightly different Planning Treatments;

### Officers' Work

This describes the most important Ceremonies involving the Inner Guard and Deacons. We will not specifically address Warden's Work, because it is assumed that anyone who has been appointed to a Warden's office will already have been a Deacon, and will therefore be familiar with the overall running of the Ceremonies. Of course, learning the Wardens' Work (and, for that matter, the Masters Work) utilises the same planning and three-stage learning system.

Because the Inner Guard and Deacon's Ceremonial work is so dominated by perambulations in the Lodge, it is really important to seek out opportunities for 'live rehearsal'. This really means Lodge of Instruction, which is covered in detail in Chapter 6. In the Degree Ceremonies, the Working Deacon is the glue which holds the Ceremony together, so it will be just about impossible to rehearse the whole Ceremony without you!

When you watch the floor-work at a Degree Ceremony,

sometimes it doesn't really look systematic. Taylors working is different from Emulation, because Taylors instructs that Officers working on the floor of the Lodge should always 'square', which makes for a more standardised Ceremony from Lodge to Lodge. This will help you when you go to watch the Ceremony in another Lodge. Emulation Ritual does not stipulate so much squaring, and so there are 'short cuts' in the floor-work. This would be fine if all Lodge rooms were the same shape and size, but they aren't, so it can be a little confusing at first view.

For the new Deacon, it's really important and very useful to break down the floor-work into its constituent parts and simplify it into stages, so you can understand and more easily memorise the sequence of events. Don't be over-awed by what you may see. It really isn't as complicated as you think.

The Junior Deacon's Work in the Initiation (First Degree) Ceremony is probably the most significant Work any Freemason will do before he reaches the Chair, for two particular reasons. Firstly, it is usually the first Ceremony in which you will play a pivotal role, so it carries some performance pressure. Secondly, and more importantly, it involves the first experience of a new Candidate in Freemasonry, which adds even more pressure. So it's in everyone's best interests that you get it right.

The Deacons Work (as in control of the Candidate) in the first two Degrees, really only contains the following elements;

- Collecting the Candidate, the Questions, the Salutes, Leaving the Lodge.

- Candidate's Re-Entrance, Salutes, and Prayer

- Some Circuits of the Temple, with Salutes and Approaches to Wardens

- Advancing from West To East, the Obligation

- Communicating the Secrets of the Degree

- Some more Circuits, with the Investiture

- Placing the Candidate

Most of these sections can be further deconstructed into their constituent actions and represented as a diagram, an example of which is shown below. To be clear, using diagrams in this way is meant only as an aid to practising the work. Your aim should be to dispose of these diagrams as soon as you are confident that you have understood the sequence of the Ceremony and your position at each stage.

In the example below, the first section of the JD's floor-work in the First Degree, the arrowed lines show your perambulations, and each numbered position corresponds with a section of Ritual. The best way to marry the Book and the Perambulations Diagram together is to mark each number in the appropriate place in the margin of your Ritual Book.

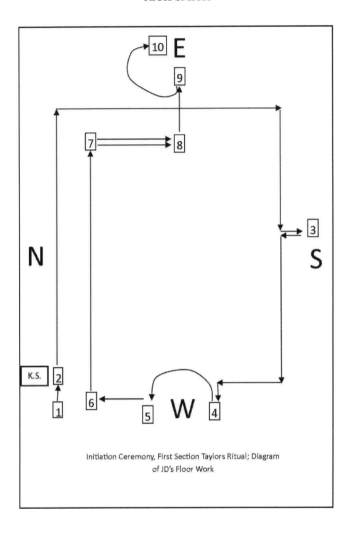

Initiation Ceremony, First Section Taylors Ritual; Diagram of JD's Floor Work

## Time Planning for Deacons

In terms of timetable planning for Deacons' work in the Degree Ceremonies, I would recommend two to three months as ideal. This is not really based on your own learning ability, but simply to allow the maximum number of practice sessions with the rest of the Team. Your timetable will largely be dictated by the Lodge of Instruction schedule, however if you have any concerns that the LoI is making assumptions (i.e. not getting started on the work early enough for you), you should politely raise your concerns with either the Preceptor or the Master, who should understand. In any case, there's nothing to stop you getting started on the work yourself, either alone, or with the assistance of a nearby friendly Brother!

Learning the Deacons' 'words' is done using exactly the same systems and processes that you will learn in the next few pages. The Ritual passages are mostly quite short, and lend themselves perfectly to a quick-learning and regular repetition system. As long as you set out your timetable clearly at the beginning, you will have no problem in getting the words right on the day.

This learning system is all about systemising and structuring the process, and that includes using Learning Aids which force you to stick to the disciplines necessary to build up to a great performance. One of the most important and easily available of these is your Mobile Phone, particularly the sophisticated alarm and reminder functions that it has. Great Ritual comes from regular repetition, and setting up daily alarms and reminders in your phone is a really easy and free way to ensure that you never forget to practice.

In addition, weekly checklists to track your rehearsal progress are also useful (example below). You can easily make these in Word or Excel, and either set them up on your PC, Tablet or Smartphone, and/or print them out and stick them in the back of your notebook, carry them in your wallet, or in your back pocket. Just check each box as many times as you practice the relevant section. This is an essential discipline, because it quickly gives you a visual representation of where you are focusing your rehearsal effort, and you can see if you are not paying enough attention to particular sections.

| Section | Mon | Tue | etc. |
|---|---|---|---|
| Part 1 Perambulations | | | |
| Approach & Dialogue to JW | | | |
| Approach & Dialogue to SW | | | |
| WM Questions to Candidate | | | |
| Advancing the Candidate to the E. | | | |
| Before & After the Obligation | | | |
| Positioning Cand. To RHS of WM | | | |
| Entrusting the Secrets | | | |
| Perambulations & Dialogue with JW | | | |
| Perambulations & Dialogue with SW | | | |
| Investing the Distinguishing Badge | | | |
| Placing the Candidate in the NE. | | | |
| The Charity Box | | | |
| The Working Tools | | | |
| Retiring from the Lodge | | | |

All these little novelties may sound a bit twee; however they are some of the Secret Weapons used by successful Ritualists, so you have nothing to lose by giving them a try.

There's not much more to say about floor-work. There are lots of ways of learning Ritual prose, but there's really only one way to achieve a high standard of floor-work, and that's Lodge of Instruction. The perambulations are taught, rather than learned.

Bear in mind that many Lodges have their own little variations on the work, and these often show up most in the floor-work. For example, some Lodges use both Deacons to change the TB's, some use only one. LoI takes care of all of this.

## The Lectures

For the purpose of this exercise, 'Lectures' include Working Tools, Charges and Tracing Board Lectures, as well the stand-alone Ceremonies such as the Long Closing, the Installation Addresses, and the Presentation of the Grand Lodge Certificate

The reason why these are separated is this; the Deacon's work involves being part of a Team, which puts a heavier dependence on the Rehearsal phase (Stage Three) and the role of Lodge of Instruction.

Conversely, the 'Lectures' are just that, and can be very effectively learned and practiced without much outside help.

You will inevitably get very bored with the notion that 'Time Is of The Essence' as it's a recurring theme throughout this book. But it really is the critical factor, so setting up a workable timetable at the beginning of the process is simply unavoidable.

## Calculating Your Time-Line

When you set about learning a Lecture, the recommended split for each of the 3 Stages is in the ratio of 2:1:1, in other words

- 2 Units of Time for Cramming & Memorising
- 1 Unit of Time for Polishing

- 1 Unit of Time for Rehearsing

In order to calculate the total length of time needed to achieve performance-grade for any Lecture, you therefore need to calculate the length of time for Stage One, Cramming, and double it.

That is done by breaking down the Lecture into sentences or passages that you can learn at the rate of one-a-day, then numbering those pieces. That tells you the number of days you will need for Stage One, and from that you can easily calculate Stages Two and Three, and the scale of the whole task.

Once again I apologise if this explanation seems banal or obvious, and indeed it probably is. However, the whole purpose of applying this method to your learning is to provide you with a structured process which you can adhere to in order to achieve the desired result Whilst you might already know how to divide by fourteen and multiply by two, you may never have thought to apply it to Learning Masonic Ritual.

Equally, once you complete the process for the first time, and prove to yourself that it works, you will then be in a position to experiment with varying the ratios between the stages, the size of the sections you apply to Stage One, and so on. Years from now, you should still be applying the same basic principles, but the numbers could be very different for each person.

Because of the variation in learning abilities across the range of people, for the purpose of this exercise we will use a 'standard model' which is Me.

You'll find a list of all the major Craft Lectures in the Appendix, with estimates of the timetable you should initially use when learning them. Of course, you will be able to adjust these schedules to suit your own abilities, but until you try one or two you won't actually know what your abilities are, so I would urge you to apply the standard model in the first instance.

For the next few Chapters, we'll be using the 'Charge After Passing' (aka The Second Degree Charge) as the example, simply to illustrate the structure of Planning. This short Ceremony is very similar in both Taylors and Emulation, two of the most common English Ritual systems. Unfortunately it does not appear in the Ritual Books of either West End or Logic working; however the principles of planning and executing are common to all monologous Ritual. For those readers who do not have the example Charge in their Lodge working, and want to follow the Planning system below, it is possible to find the Charge After Passing in various places on the internet. At time of writing, an accurate example is to be found at www.stichtingargus.nl

This Charge is an ideal piece for the aspiring Ritualist, because not only is it beautifully written, containing many rhythms and cues, but it naturally breaks down into fourteen bite-sized 'chunks' which are the perfect size to be memorized in two weeks at the rate of one-a–day.

Applying the Three-Stage Process (CPR) explained earlier, and the Standard Model (Me!) this works as follows;

1. Stage One (Cramming); 14 Days

2. Stage Two (Polishing); 7 Days

3. Stage Three (Rehearsing); 7 Days

So we will make a plan that involves learning the example to 'performance standard' in One Month.

### Milestones

The purpose of setting up a detailed timetable at the beginning is to give yourself fixed points so that you can measure your progress.

Once you've 'locked in' to a precise plan, you've automatically created your milestones, targets to shoot for which will keep you on schedule to peak at the right time; the day of the Meeting. You might mark the Stage One milestones in your Ritual Book, or make another little table similar to the one above. Alternately you could place calendar entries in your Schedule on your smartphone or computer, with count-down alerts in the couple of days before each milestone. Choose the method that is most likely to get your attention!

Once you start, you'll soon find out if your milestones are realistic. You can adapt your on-going approach once you see how fast it's working for you.

## Understanding the Ritual

A lot has been written about this, and it is obviously important. But here we're mainly concerned with things that will enable you to learn quickly and deliver competently. Your intimate relationship with the Work will only really gather momentum once you are through the first couple of performances.

I mentioned previously that the Craft Ritual is largely metaphorical, in so much as the messages behind the stories are the main elements of Masonic and moral improvement, rather than the stories themselves. The use of metaphors to deliver implicit benefits is a key plank of Neuro Linguistic Programming (NLP) and Hypnotherapy. The human mind is very sophisticated in the way it deals with language, and is highly capable of extracting and applying the meanings behind metaphors.

Of course, to try and decipher the meanings behind the Ritual is another science entirely, and really not relevant to what we are targeting here, which is the learning and delivery of the Ritual itself. Besides, we're concentrating on the value of the language, which more than stands up on its own.

Masonry is constantly evolving to keep pace with people's changing lives, in order to avoid diminution and marginalisation. What goes on in the Lodge must remain beautiful and elegant, and the core tenets must be respected and preserved. However, if we are going to retain our beautiful Ritual, and grow our Membership, I believe that we need to find attractive ways of engaging with the Work so that younger men can appreciate it and perform it well.

So, the simple approach is to apply an entry-level standard of understanding, sufficient to enable you to work through the process of learning the Work. Basically, if it makes sense to you when you read it through, you probably have enough understanding to learn it! In time, all will become clear.

Phew, I think that covers the preamble. Now it's time to get started on the Work.

## Stage One; 'Cramming'

The 'First Regular Step' in this system of learning to perform Ritual involves 'Cramming' at the beginning, even if it's just a rough version of your work.

You can polish the language later (hardy anyone ever gets it 100% right) but it's important to demonstrate to yourself that you can fit the bulk of the language around the Ceremony. Later, you might try visualising stories when you get to the Tracing Boards, but in your early offices, you simply need to concentrate on linking short passages of Ritual with well-executed perambulations, crisp salutes, and strong guidance for the Candidate.

This initial Objective is to get yourself quickly to a situation where you can stumble right through the Ceremony in your head. If you can, towards the end of Stage One, you really need to go and see it done again so it will all start to fit together. The techniques for this initial cramming are covered in Chapter 4.

## Chapter 3 Summary

- To start, find somewhere that you can go to watch a performance of the Ceremony you are learning.

- There are Three Stages; Cramming, Polishing, and Rehearsing (C.P.R.)

- There are two kinds of Work; Officer's Work and Lectures, which require slightly differing approaches.

- For Officer's floor-work, break it down into sections. Use diagrams to help you rehearse the perambulations.

- Set up daily alarms on your cellphone to practice your words.

- Carry a rehearsal check-list to keep you on schedule.

- Break down the Lectures into small portions that you can memorise at the rate of one-per-day. Count the days, and double it for the total time you'll need before you perform it. If you can, add two weeks for contingencies.

# 4
# LEARNING AND MEMORIZING:
## STAGE ONE 'CRAMMING'

In this Chapter, we will a lay out simple system for memorising a Ceremony for the first time, and get you started.

The primary objective is to 'Cram' the memorising task as quickly as possible in order to give yourself maximum time for Polishing the Work in Stage 2, and then Rehearsing the Delivery in Stage 3

Some studies appear to show that memory is actually a holistic process across the whole of the brain, which takes and processes feeds from different senses. The notion exists that it's something like a database; when something happens to you, the sensory inputs are split out and stored in their appropriate brain areas. So all the visual stuff gets stored in the sight area, the sounds go to the audio area, and various kinesthetic strands such as temperature, texture, pleasure, pain and so on are stored in their appropriate places.

When some kind of memory trigger occurs, such as a

question or query, the *medial pre-frontal cortex* sets about re-associating all the sensory strands and calling them up, to rebuild the memory. This could account for the condition where you try to recall something but have to concentrate for a few seconds before you can get a clear picture. It takes time for the brain to find all the right pieces.

## Memory Recall

Learning Ritual is predominately about Memory, or more importantly, Recall.

We need to import accurate information, using whatever method ensures that the information is stored in a usable form. Then we need to be able to retrieve it, quickly, and in the right order. To do this well, we need to learn how to trust our powers of recall. The more we use recall, the stronger it will become, just like muscle training.

There are dozens of books on training your memory, but for our purposes we will use a really simple and easy technique to train and learn to trust our recall powers.

You're now going to dive right in and start memorising your work, using a structure which will tell you exactly what you need to do, every day. Your key objective is to memorise the Work, so you will be reciting parts of the Ritual, both silently and out-loud, a lot.

Each time you hit a bump in the road, your immediate temptation will be to reach for the Book. That's a reflex action, but it's the wrong thing to do, because it holds back your commitment to really trusting your own abilities.

Use a little routine to head-off that reflex action. Whilst you are learning and reciting, every time you forget a word or lose your way, you should do the following;

- Place your finger to your lips

- Pause for (about) ten seconds, whilst you...

- Dig deep inside to retrieve the lost word or phrase

At first it will only work occasionally, but as you progress you might be surprised at how you improve your hit-rate. As you get better at it, you won't need the whole ten seconds. If you can get better than three seconds by the end of the process, you should be able to beat your Prompter most of the time!

Co-incidentally the same gesture crops up in Royal Arch Ritual, as a trigger to 'Remember Your Obligation'.

It's very important that you use a physical 'quietener' to kick-off a recall event which is why we use the finger to the lips, because most people associate it with quietness. It's also a gesture that won't draw any attention if you do it on a bus or a train! You can substitute one of your own if you like.

Use this technique all the time whilst you are learning the Ritual, so that it becomes automatic. Training your recall is important if you want to master performance-level Ritual. It's easy, and it's free, so start using it right away.

## Photographic Memory

Everyone's heard about the fabled 'photographic memory'. It's true; some people can recall a detailed map or plan after only the briefest view. I recently saw a video on Facebook about an autistic teenager who went on a helicopter flight over New York, then immediately drew a detailed aerial view of Manhattan Island, on a canvas about ten metres wide!

Of course these people are rare; however it appears that most people are blessed with some degree of visual recall ability which can be developed, and it will develop on its own if it's used properly.

Among the weapons in your Ritual armoury, you will, over time, subconsciously store the position of words and phrases on the pages of your Ritual Book. I have found that the phrases which are particularly memorable are the ones which run across from one page to another, particularly the bottom of a left hand page to the top of a right hand page. This type of recall can be useful in remembering the sequence of paragraphs.

## How Much Time?

In the previous Chapter, we calculated that four weeks looks like a reasonable timetable to get this Charge ready, though I would always recommend that you add two weeks contingency to anything you take on for the first time.

You've learned how to break down the passages into natural sections which are easy to learn within a structure. The key to Cramming is short bursts of focused activity, utilising automated cues to trigger you to practice.

The most important thing is to get cracking on it straight away. On no account should you procrastinate. You know the task, so now you need to put your plan into action.

## Why Cramming Works Best

As we introduced earlier, this learning method requires you to memorise the complete Ritual passage as your first priority. This then gives you the maximum time to polish and rehearse the whole Ceremony, so that all the parts are equally ingrained into your memory.

The alternative, which you may have tried, is to learn it sequentially, pacing out the major sections over the whole time leading up to the meeting. You may have perfected the early sections, but if your timetable slips at all you might not get to the last few sections until just before the Meeting. This means you may have learned the first two thirds really well, but you're taking a huge risk because you haven't spent anywhere near as much time on the last part. You will often see the result of this method in a Lodge, when the performance is perfect at the beginning but starts needing prompts in the last section.

So the sole objective of this first phase is to memorise the passage in rough form as quickly as possible. Of course, different people will have different capacities for memorising, and different calls on their time, but in general it would be reasonable to memorise a small paragraph each day, somewhere between twenty and forty words.

### Example: The Charge After Passing (Second Degree)

This example, being a Charge, is actually a sequence of 'instructions' to the Candidate. You can easily transpose it into a bulleted or numbered list, which you will find contains thirteen or fourteen (depending on your Ritual system) separate and distinct pieces of prose. There are just less than three hundred words, so it will easily break down to shorter passages of digestible length.

This lends itself perfectly to a two-week Cramming Effort. You will take one of these sections each day, and learn it. Some days the passage will be quite short; that's fine, you might decide you can take on more than one that day, but whatever the case, you will discipline yourself to tackle one new part each day, so that you have completed the rough learning within the first fortnight.

Remember, this Charge After Passing is our study example. If you have other specific Work you are planning to learn, just split it down the same way and set your timetable according to the 2:1:1 ratio we explained earlier.

### Setting Up a Daily Routine

So, you have your outline plan for the first phase. How do you now ensure that each daily section goes in and stays in, so that the parts build into a whole?

### Morning Routine

For most people, their mind is most receptive and agile within the first few minutes of waking up in the morning.

The best time to memorise something verbal and new is first thing in the morning, before the distractions of the normal day start to get in the way.

You probably get your best 'alone time' first thing in the morning, maybe in the bathroom. This is Prime Time for Ritual learning. Even if you struggle to fit in your learning during the rest of the day, you should focus on this early 'session' as a priority. Have your Book with you, or a copy of the short piece you are learning for the day, and read it through.

## Silent versus Out Loud

Reciting out loud is always best. It acts on more than one sensory channel in your brain, and also introduces breathing and tonality at an early stage. You should actively look for opportunities to learn and rehearse out loud, though of course it might not be convenient all the time. It becomes more important in the later stages of the process, and by the time you are getting close to the Meeting you will be strongly encouraged to fully rehearse out loud at least once each day.

However, in the early stages you can practice silently as long as you focus. Even just mouthing the words as you try to memorise them will be an improvement over doing it all in your head.

You're only trying to deal with one sentence or phrase at a time, before you move on to the next one. In the next chapter, we're going to look at some tricks to help you memorise those complex little phrases that don't automatically sit well in your brain.

Take no more than ten minutes on this first exercise of the day, but try to absorb a meaningful piece of the passage, maybe a complete sentence or two. Whilst you're still holding your book, look away and see if you can recite it. If you stumble, don't immediately go back to the Book. Just place your finger to your lips, concentrate for a few seconds and see if you can recall the part you are missing. This is an important discipline to teach yourself, because if you are struggling during the rehearsal phase, or even on the day of the performance, this skill of digging down and reconstructing (recalling) the words will be your safety-net, and it's definitely one of the Secret Weapons of a Great Ritualist.

Don't expect it to work straight away; you need to train your mind a little before you'll be able to execute 'cold recall' every time. So don't get frustrated with yourself if it takes more than a few tries before you can recite a sentence or paragraph all the way through. And especially don't worry if you're confused over the order or sequence of words in the passage; we're going to clean up the details later.

The important thing is to keep trying to recite this single short passage until you get it, just once, and it makes sense.

Once you've managed to recite that section once, from beginning to end, even if it's a little uncertain or out of sequence, put the book face down. This is a good time to get into the shower.

### Finding Anchors

When you are learning Ritual, you will find that some sentences and phrases are easy to retain, and some just take much longer. One technique which helps is to use the easily-memorised pieces as a type of 'anchor'. In this context, an anchor is a safe-place which allows you to periodically centre yourself in the learning process and eventually in the delivery. Once you've recognised a few anchors you will begin to have a spatial impression of the piece as a whole, and you can put your concentration into dealing with the trickier parts in-between.

As you progress, you will use larger anchors. Whole paragraphs and (in the case of the Masters Work) whole monologues become anchors, because you can recite them on auto-pilot.

Find a few anchors for yourself, early in the process. Read the ceremony, and pick out any words or phrases which 'speak to you'. Think about them, and look at their position on the page. Once you have a few, you just need to join the dots.

### Quick Summary

So that's the basic structure of memorising the Ritual, sentence by sentence. You will always use this method first, even when you get better at re-learning a Ceremony you've done before. You're ready for learning and memorising sequences.

To Summarise;

- Take one sentence at a time.

- Read it over again, until you are ready to try to recite it.

- If that works, keep reciting as often as you can.

- If you get stuck, place your finger to your lips and focus on trying to recall it for about 10 seconds

- If you need to, check the Book and repeat the cycle

- Don't move on until you have mastered that sentence or phrase.

So let's put it into action.

### Day One; Kick-Starting Your Plan

On Day One, which ideally should be the very next day after you have been allocated (or simply decided for yourself) the Work, we are setting you a very achievable target, which is the first sentence, no more than fifteen to twenty words.

Follow the instructions above, and you should have it done in the first half hour of the day. If you're practicing in the shower or the bath, just keep going, even when you think you've learned it, until you have to do something else which requires your concentration. If you find yourself struggling with a piece of text, dig deep inside your memory and try to recall it. Don't let yourself get frustrated, just follow the sequence. If you absolutely cannot recall it, check the Book again. Alternate as many times as you need, but by the time you unlock the bathroom door, you should have most of it in place. Now go and get your breakfast!

## Make Appointments with Yourself

It's helpful if you keep silently rehearsing it. If you're alone, that might be perfectly OK. But if it's inconvenient simply drop it from your front-of-mind.

Don't worry, that short burst of intense focus and activity has set up a chain reaction in your subconscious, and the process will continue in the background without you having to focus on it. Just get on with your normal day, but before you forget, book yourself an Appointment.

Set yourself a short time-slot to revisit your learning at a convenient time of the day when you can guarantee you will not be distracted. Maybe you're going to drive to work, which is ideal because you can speak out loud if you're alone in the car. Or maybe you're catching the bus or train. It doesn't matter; just tell yourself that at a certain time, in a certain situation "I am going to check myself".

The best way to enforce this timetable is to use your mobile phone's Alarm function. Try putting some silent alarms in your phone so you don't forget to keep the appointments. It's that simple and you really don't need much time, but make sure you repeat it two or three times a day in the beginning.

If you have a Smart Phone you can set multiple alarms which will repeat at the same time every day. You can usually tag each alarm you set, so you can add a reminder of what you need to do. When the alarm triggers, it will put a notification reminder on your screen.

You can write quite long tags, so you can be quite detailed with your reminders. Once you set up the alarms, your practice timetable is on auto-pilot. This is a really powerful but very simple tool that anyone can do with very little effort.

Maybe you are going to be really busy and distracted until lunch-time, so set up your appointment accordingly. You only need three or four minutes to check yourself, but it's important that you stick to the timing. If you miss it, or forget, just set up another appointment as soon as you remember, and so on. The objective here is to check yourself regularly during the course of the day, so that by the time you get home in the evening you will have correctly memorised the passage of that day.

Be prepared, you may find yourself perfectly able to recite the piece at lunch-time but you've completely forgotten it by tea-time! This is normal, it happens to the best of us, and it is nothing to worry about. You haven't actually forgotten anything. You've just caught yourself out by trying to access something from a part of your memory that it has not yet penetrated, but the piece is in your mental 'system'. Check your book. Of course, you knew it all along; don't beat yourself up over it, it's all going to fall into place if you just stick to the system!

Try to fit in at least three of these little appointments during the day. The number of appointments you can achieve each day will have a directly proportional effect on the speed at which you memorise the Work.

A good time to do your last 'daylight check' is just before you get home. Because for most people, once you cross the threshold from work-mode to home-mode, there's a whole new set of demands on your time. Family always comes first. So, if your final check was OK, you can shelve your learning until later.

Relax and let your mind do the hard work in the background.

### Don't Try To Learn In the Evening

I don't really advocate setting aside time in the evening (so called 'me time') to learn Ritual. Sure, it works for some people, but it seems to fail for most people, and it never worked for me! That's not to say that evenings are off-limits, but it's 'free study' time if you like. There's no evening homework!

In the evening, especially after a day at work, tiredness and concentration are a major factor. In addition, there are numerous distractions in most people's environments, like kids, dinner, TV, visitors, and other family responsibilities. Besides, if you follow this system, you shouldn't actually need to 'set time aside' because this method of learning is designed to fit into your everyday routine without disruption.

### Having a Drink?

I'd be a hypocrite if I tried to persuade you to change any of your personal habits in the name of learning Masonic Ritual. This learning system is specifically designed to fit around your everyday life, not to force you to change your habits; after all, it's just a hobby. Nobody's going to die if you get it wrong, and you're not going to get paid if you get it right, so relax.

However, remember this; although it is perfectly possible to rehearse, repeat and recite *learned* information after a few drinks, it is extremely difficult to learn and retain *new* information. That's one of the reasons why learning the new stuff is so much more effective in the morning.

**Evenings Are For Relaxing**

To repeat, there's no obligation for you to think about the Work during the evening, as long as you stick to the morning, daytime and night time routines.

But there's nothing to stop you practicing in the evening either. Everyone needs to go to the bathroom from time to time, so there are probably two or three little down-time opportunities for you to mentally or verbally recite pieces of your work. The evening is a good time to separate out any particularly troubling sentences or 'lists' that need extra repetition.

Some years ago, when I was first learning about Hypnosis, I spent a week at a seminar with Paul McKenna, the famous TV hypnotist, and Richard Bandler, the founder of NLP (neuro-linguistic programming). During one of the workshops I asked Paul McKenna 'do' hypnosis on me to make me leave my living room every time Eastenders came on TV, and do something more useful. In a matter of seconds the change was made, and it still works every time after nearly ten years!

This demonstrates the power of triggers or cues, as auto-suggestions to take some action. At the beginning it is worth setting your own trigger, something like my Eastenders theme tune, to designate time when you could be doing something more useful, like practicing your Ritual! It's just a small commitment you make, which is easy to stick to because it makes total sense. If you make sure you follow your trigger a few times, it will quickly become a habit and you too will be doing something useful.

Again, as long as you follow the core tasks in the system,

which is to rehearse small things regularly throughout the day, you'll be in good shape by the time you get to bed-time.

## Bed-Time Rehearsal

It's been said that Masonic Ritual is a great cure for insomnia. I can personally testify to the truth of that statement. It's right up there with Counting Sheep!

Just as the first half-hour of the day is the best time to implant new information, so is the last half-hour the ideal time to cement and solidify the 'Day's Work'. This is a major pillar in your learning system so it's important that you commit to it.

Try this sequence, which is specifically designed so that you can fit it in with your normal night-time routine, also involving another visit to the bathroom!

First, check your learning for the day. This could be while you are brushing your teeth, since this largely precludes you from talking to anyone! Just make sure that you have memorised what you planned to learn at least 90% accurately, for that day. The same rules apply; if you are struggling, go down inside and try to use your memory recall to reconstruct the missing parts. If that fails, check the Book. The objective is to be clear, by the time you turn out the lights, so that the last thing you do before you sleep is to mentally recite your Work.

This is the perfect time for solidifying and confirming learned information. As you descend into the dreamy somnambulist state just before sleep, you are mimicking hypnosis, which is an ideal state for learning. Just lie there and practice your words, in your head. In the dark, without distraction, you will be able to find a focus and concentration which is often difficult to achieve during the day, so this is a very valuable time for the Ritualist.

People sometimes say "but I have so much on my mind".

Well, you'll have to switch your priorities for a few minutes. Sorry, but even with this system, there is some sacrifice required!

Right from the early days of learning a passage, as you build the pieces, sentence by sentence and phrase by phrase, you'll probably find that the tranquillising effect will have you sleeping like a baby before you get to the end.

Whatever the case, that final few minutes of silent mental repetition should complete your day's learning and set you up nicely for…

## Day 2

So, you wake up on the morning of Day 2.

We already established a system for you to learn the day's passage, but first you need to confirm that yesterday's piece is still in there. If it's vague, you have the tools at your disposal; first try memory recall. If that doesn't work, check the Book. Practice yesterday's piece a few times, just to connect the dots in your memory again. Assuming you are now comfortable, which if you have followed the system so far you will be, we're ready to move on.

There's nothing different about the way you're going to memorise the next sentence or paragraph. What is most important is to learn it as a stand-alone piece.

Just do exactly the same as yesterday. Read it through as many times as it takes to be able to start to recite it, then check, re-check, recall, and eventually put the book down and jump in the shower. What worked for you yesterday is going to work for you today, just the same, so you can be confident that you are well on the way to memorising the whole Ceremony.

But there's a difference today; once you have a basic grasp of this second piece of Work (and remember we're not concerned with detail at this stage) you can, when you're ready, put the two pieces together.

Now, this might frustrate you a little for the first few tries, but persevere. Remember; you KNOW the Work from yesterday. What may happen is that, just when you think you've got a handle on today's work, you try to out the two pieces together and although you can easily repeat section one, the new stuff just evaporates when you get to it. That's no problem. Again, use your memory recall, because it's in there somewhere and you just need to find it. Check the Book as a final resort whenever you get really stuck, but put it down each time and force yourself to dig deep in your memory.

It's a building exercise. Each time you repeat it, you will improve. After a little while you'll get it right for the first time, and then you'll start getting it right every time. It's a process.

Your objective before you start your day properly is to be able to recite the two pieces together, with 90% accuracy.

As with Day One, you need to make those little appointments with yourself, so set the alarms on your phone. These will nudge you into your learning zone without you having to make a decision. It works, so please use it. The more we can automate the process, the more effective it will be.

We talked before about your evening routine, which probably varies a lot from day-to-day, but you'll now have a good idea about your own capabilities, so you can tune your rehearsal schedule up or down to accommodate yourself. The key milestones are the mornings. You shouldn't move on until you're 90% solid on the previous day's Work.

Occasionally, you may miss a milestone and you won't be ready to move on to the next passage, so don't. Just add another day to yesterday's Work and make sure you've got it. You have a couple of extra days built into your schedule, but please try to keep up with your original plan. There's no such thing as too much rehearsal time, as you'll learn in the later stages...

Follow the pattern as closely as possible each day; that is

- First 5 Minutes; Quick revision of yesterday's learning, checking that it's still there and checking the book to bring it back. Put it aside

- Start working on today's section, following the same memorisation technique

- When you're ready, try the whole passage.

- Set up your micro-alarms for your three daytime rehearsal slots.

- Make your last 'daylight check' before you settle into your evening activity.

- Take little opportunities to recite the work during the evening, if you can.

- At bed-time, check yourself before lights out, and then rehearse in your mind whilst you fall asleep.

### Onwards and Upwards

By Day Three you should be getting the hang of this method and feel it working for you. The most important thing about this first stage is to stay focused on the memorising process, so that you quickly assemble the complete passage. To repeat, we are not so concerned about the detail, the little link words, or even the order of word sequence at this early stage. What is most important is to get the sentences and paragraphs in the correct order.

Once you are two or three days in, you have proven to yourself that you have the intellectual faculties to learn this kind of prose, so you should have no lack of confidence going forwards. It becomes a mechanical process which you can re-use every time you learn.

Of course as you gradually build up the passage, your rehearsal time will expand. This is not a problem. The Charge after Passing only takes around two minutes to deliver, so finding a few slots during the day should present no problem.

## The Half Way Point

When you arrive at the half-way point of this memorisation (at the end of the first week) we will adopt a modified strategy. It's important to give the whole Ceremony equal attention. As I mentioned earlier you'll regularly see Ceremonies which start out brilliantly but deteriorate towards the end. This is usually because the person has used a purely linear structure for their learning. They may have rehearsed the first half of the Ceremony for several weeks, but the last part only got a few days at the end.

At this early stage you shouldn't try to manage sections of Ritual more than one page in length at a time. So, in the example of this Charge After Raising that's a simple division as it is two pages long.

Once you've done the first page, you're going to mentally box it off, and treat the second half of the Ceremony as an entirely separate piece. This breakdown gives you a big advantage when you're learning, and also adds an additional memory aid into your toolbox for later.

We're certainly not going to discard the first section, because if you don't tend to it, it will start to decay. The first section will be the first thing you mentally rehearse when you wake up in the morning, and the first thing you mentally recite when you put the lights out at bed time. You will keep working it, ensuring that it becomes more and more natural to you. But you won't try to join it up with the second half until you have finished memorising that separately.

These 'Page Breaks' will ensure that you give enough focus and attention to the second half of the Ceremony, so that when you do finally connect the two halves, you know them more or less equally. Then the entire rehearsal phase will be balanced, and this will be repeated in your performance.

You can (for example) break down Tracing Boards in the same way, except that these Lectures have distinct sections rather than being one long piece separated only by pages. Looking forwards, an example of a Learning Plan for the Second Degree Tracing Board might look something like the example below.

If you make a checklist like this for your Work, by marking each time you run through a section in the daily boxes, you can easily see which parts are being neglected, so that you give every section equal attention through the week.

With the Charges, we can more easily break the detail of the Ceremony into numbered paragraphs, as explained earlier, whereas Tracing Board Lectures have a different structure.

Rehearsal Checklist for Second Tracing Board:

| Section | Mon | Tue | etc. |
|---|---|---|---|
| When the Temple at Jerusalem… | | | |
| The height of these P's… | | | |
| They were set up as… | | | |
| At the building of KST… | | | |
| The Word … takes its rise… | | | |
| To render his victory decisive… | | | |
| Our Ancient Brethren… | | | |
| Three rule a Lodge… | | | |
| 5 Noble Orders of Architecture | | | |
| 7 Liberal Arts & Sciences | | | |
| When Our Ancient Brethren… | | | |

## Down-Time Opportunities

Most people have lots of small opportunities to do a little Ritual practice. How many of these would work for you?

- In the bathroom
- Walking to the bus stop or rail station
- Waiting for the bus or train
- On the bus, on the train
- Instead of reading a magazine
- Eating your breakfast or lunch
- In a queue

- Driving the car
- Doctor's waiting room
- The Dentist Chair (this one is brilliant)
- In a taxi
- Exercising in the gym
- Cycling or Jogging
- Walking the dog
- Washing the car

To master the memorisation phase, you'll need to commit yourself to at least a few of these opportunities. Think about it in terms of using dead time for something useful, and it will start to deliver big benefits.

## The Sum of the Parts

In our example, The Charge After Passing, you broke down the Ritual into short sentences or paragraphs and learned them one by one. In addition, you broke down the whole passage into two one-page halves. If you have done those correctly, followed the system, and stuck to your timetable and milestones, you should have all the parts committed to memory in about two weeks.

Now it's time to put the two halves together, and try your first full-length run through.

Remember we're not looking for perfection yet. But when you put it all together for the first time it should begin to make some kind of logical sense. As we said at the beginning, a Charge is basically a set of instructions to the Candidate. You might remember the sequence because you used a numbering system from the start, which is fine. Alternately, you may have memorised each sentence in terms of how it follows on from the one before it.

However you have done it, Congratulations. That's the

hardest part. You've assembled the ingredients. Next we'll start to focus on Stage Two, when you'll polish and perfect the language, and cook the whole dish.

**Chapter 4 Summary.**

- The Objective is to Cram or Memorize the Work to 90% accuracy, as quickly as possible.

- Set up your Morning Routine as the best time to start the new Work for the day.

- Focus on using Memory Recall before you reach for the Book.

- Set up a Daily Practice Routine, using Alarms on your phone.

- Recite Out Loud whenever possible, for maximum benefit.

- Relax in the Evening, but do a little practice whenever you get an opportunity

- Set up Cues and Triggers to 'do something useful'.

- Use Bed-Time as the best time to silently rehearse.

- Break the whole Work into page-size sections so you learn each section equally.

- Use a paper 'Checklist' to plot your progress and balance your efforts.

- Find small 'down-time' opportunities to fit in a little practice.

- Remember; the more you do, the quicker you'll complete Stage One.

# 5
# STAGE TWO: POLISHING THE WORK

Now that you have completed the Cramming stage, you should be able to recite the whole Ceremony from start to finish, even if you're not completely verbatim. The objective of Stage One was to get the language into your memory by whatever means possible, so that you have the raw material to start building your eventual performance.

In this second Stage, you are going to take what you have and work on the detail. The key objective now is to nurture the Ceremony or Lecture, and achieve the following;

- Finally memorise an authentic version, ideally the same as the Book.

- Incorporate rhythm, anchors, cues and lists, so that it becomes natural to you.

- Practice constantly, until the recital becomes technically automatic and you no longer have to think about the words you are saying.

- Use different techniques to check yourself and build your confidence.

## Filling In the Detail

As we have seen, it's not so important to nail the details right at the beginning. A good metaphor is that of a Sculptor making a bust from stone. He starts off with a plain block of marble, but very early in the process it will start to resemble a head and shoulders. Later, he will Work on refining the shape, then the texture of each part, the skin, the bone structure, the hair and so on. Only in the last stage will he finalise the details, perhaps the eyes, which add the personality and recognition to the piece.

Let's assume that you have completed the rough memorisation your Work, or maybe our example Second Degree Charge in around two weeks. Now we enter a new phase, which is to refine the language so that it synchronises with the Book. In this part of the process, there are numerous techniques you can employ to help you. Once again, we put a time limit on ourselves, because it's important to get to the final Rehearsal stage with plenty of time to spare.

Now we're checking what you have memorised, and correcting the language. We'll assume that you have understood the language and general meaning of the Ritual you are learning. By now, if there are any abbreviations or terms which are unclear to you, you should have asked someone for an explanation.

## Maintaining Your Practice Routines

Earlier in the process, you were shown how to set-up specific routines to ensure you made small time-investments in the Ritual every day. Ideally, you are using the Alarm function on your phone to remind you when it's time to do a few minutes Work. By now this structure should be working well for you. It shows that if you apply some direct focus for a few minutes each time, you create a subconscious momentum which keeps working in the background. Each time you come to check up on yourself, you've moved forwards without consciously trying.

It's ideal if you can maintain the same 'appointments' each day. However, you need to use the time in different ways, so you might need to re-organise your Ritual schedule a little bit.

## Hands-Free versus Hands-On

Some of the time, you can be 'Hands Free'. This means you are simply reciting your Work without necessarily referring to the Book or any other copy of the Ritual. This is pure practice time, and it's really important because now you are closer to having an authentic version of the Work at your fingertips. You're using spaced repetition to improve your familiarity with the piece, which will help with your confidence in the final Stage.

At other times you will need to be more 'Hands On', using some of the following techniques to audit and check your progress, and create additional learning tools for yourself.

It's important to keep your morning 'Bathroom Routine' going. You'll recall that we identified first thing in the day as the optimum time to learn new information. It's also a good time to revise what you did the day before. In the early morning, your brain is at full power and you aren't pre-occupied by the accumulating distractions that build up during the course of a normal day.

Your morning routine in Stage 2 is a simple recital session, either silently or, if you can do it, out loud. Whilst you go through your routine, just make little mental notes of any places where you're still unsure of what you are reciting. If you like, you can put pencil marks in your Ritual Book, and then erase them as you fix each variance.

Your bed-time routine is completely 'Hands Free'. If you've been following this structure for your memorisation phase, you should be getting the benefits from this session, both in terms of cementing the Ritual into your memory, and helping you to get off to sleep! So keep going with that last mental recital each night.

The most important thing in this Polishing phase is that you actually notice that you are eliminating errors and glitches each morning and evening. Accuracy and fluency are the key attributes you are aiming to develop in this Stage.

## Hands-On Polishing

Next, you'll read about some practical tools and techniques that you can use to really boost your accuracy and familiarity with the Work. These require a little bit more effort, so you need to be able to find some hands-on time. If you can manage thirty minutes every other day, you should be able to master your Work within the time allotted for this Phase.

Remember, this section is targeting accuracy and precision, and really is all about repetition. Each time you go through your Work without relying on a printed or recorded copy, you are embedding it deeper and deeper into your learned memory bank. You might not fully appreciate this the first time you learn it, but it will be much simpler when you get a chance to use it for the second time.

## A Word about Boredom

Learning Ritual can get boring occasionally. It starts out challenging, but after you have repeated the same piece of language a few dozen times (or even a few hundred times, when you move on to the bigger passages) you may start to feel a bit fed up with it.

Understand that boredom is a positive outcome at this stage. It implies that you've successfully memorised your Work, and that remembering and reciting has ceased to trouble or even challenge you. So turn it to your advantage. When you feel too bored to do your two or three minutes of rehearsal, push yourself to try for a 'perfect recital' in order to prove to yourself how brilliant you are. Then, instead of feeling bored and guilty that you skipped a session, you can feel smug and cocky that you did it with one hand tied behind your back!

Whatever you do, don't succumb to the boredom and be tempted to stop or slow down. It's a temporary thing, which will pass. The trick is to have a clear vision of the target you are shooting for, which is to give a good performance in the Lodge. That will definitely not be boring!

So, maintain the momentum by sticking to your daily routine, something like;

- Morning (bathroom) routine; Up to ten minutes full recital (that's long enough for a whole Tracing Board) without the Book

- Morning Commute; Silent recital on public transport, checking yourself after each section. Alternately, recital out-loud if you're alone in the car.

- Lunch-Time; try to fit in a read-through or some type-checking if you can. Every couple of days is enough, as long as you focus.

- Final 'Daylight Check'; review any 'upgrades'; you've made that day, making sure you have definitely incorporated them into your mental 'Master Copy'

- Take the evening off. There are more important things than Masonry. (Unless it's Lodge of Instruction)

- Bed-Time; Your final run-through of the day. A good time to start visualising the actual Ceremony, particularly mentally practicing the perambulations if you need to.

# THE TECHNIQUES IN STAGE TWO

## Sequences of Words (Lists)

Many Ritual passages have 'lists' inside, such as the Five Noble Orders Of Architecture, The Seven Liberal Arts and Sciences, the Four Cardinal Virtues and so on. Some people have the kind of memory which enables them to memorise these short sequences easily, others do not. Learning lists is just another technique, and if you separate these tricky sequences out, you can learn them much more easily. When you perform the Ritual, confident recital of the 'lists' are important. They form anchors to the whole piece.

These sequences are also important because many Brethren in the Lodge, whilst having forgotten or never learned the Ritual you are performing, will have unconsciously memorised these sequences as a result of having heard them many times. So it's important not only to get the words correct, but also to get them in the correct order. Everyone will be mentally prompting you!

So if you have ever struggled with these sequences, it's a good idea to separate them out and learn them as standalone items, and the ideal time to do this is in the middle of Stage Two.

In the current example, the Charge after Passing, here are the Lists;

- Judge with candour,

- admonish with friendship, (and)

- reprehend with mercy.

and

- improve your intellectual powers,

- qualify yourself to become a useful member of society and,

- like a skilful brother, strive to excel in what is good and great.

and

- encourage industry (and)

- reward merit,

- supply the wants (and)

- relieve the necessities

There are some tips and tricks for using abbreviations and other memory cues later on, but for now it is sufficient to remember that these sequences should be separated out and learned in isolation, after which they will re-integrate back into your learning quite smoothly.

## Visualisation?

Visualisation is a useful tool if you are mentally rehearsing Officer's Work involving perambulations.

Some people recommend you use visualisation to learn the spoken Ritual itself. I'm on the fence about this; I understand and appreciate the value of visualisation because it is used to great effect in Sports Psychology, Hypnotherapy, and even Guided Meditation. I previously suggested it as a technique that can be used in very small and focused doses in the Memorisation or Cramming Phase.

But in terms of a learning aid for Ritual text, I think that for many people it just adds an extra unwanted step.

In his book 'Ritual in Mind', Graham Chisnell lays out a memory system for Learning Masonic Ritual Tools using Visualisation as its central plank, should you feel inclined to explore this method for yourself.

## 'List' Learning Tips and Tricks

- Learn Lists separately, and then integrate them into the main passage.

- Find acronyms to jog your memory

- Learn your Lists early. Use them as anchor points and links when you learn the passage.

Acronyms are a great way to remember lists. Visualisation is a valid technique for some people. Numbered lists work for others. The most important thing is to learn lists separately to the passage, and use your 'list competence' as an anchor point in the whole Ceremony.

## Link words

In listening to Ritual what regularly come up are errors related to the almost inconsequential small words which link all the big words together. Tenses, genders and so on are often overlooked in learning Ritual, usually because has not enough time was allowed for this middle 'Polishing' phase.

The easiest way to approach this is by a gradual process of correction. Once you have the rough passage committed to memory, just read through it in the Book and you will easily notice the places where you may be using an incorrect word or phrase. It's then a simple matter to recite that part of the Ritual and check that you are now using the right word (for example an 'and' instead of an 'or'). The next time you run through the full passage, you'll mentally remind yourself to use the new correct word when you reach that point. After two or three run-throughs, the new word or words are seamlessly integrated into your mental 'Master Copy' of the passage.

To summarise this simple technique;

- Recite a good-sized portion of your Work

- Read through it again (out loud) from the Book

- Your errors will be usually be obvious

- Run over those sentences three or four times

- Recite the passage again

- If necessary, rinse and repeat!

Again, we're not looking for absolute perfection, because there are other techniques that will help to clean up any remaining errors. However, you should aim to be better than 95% accurate before you move on.

For the more ambitious Ritualist, this is a useful skill to master in case you find yourself switching between two different Ritual conventions (for example Taylors and Emulation) if you are a guest in another Lodge. The little variances make a big difference, especially to the audience.

## Acronyms and Abbreviations

The Ritual is scattered with small phrases which act as triggers for a paragraph or passage. There are good examples to be found in the Obligations in the Degree Ceremonies.

An Obligation is for the Candidate to be led through a series of promises about what he will or will not do as a result of having been admitted to a particular Degree. Throughout the Three Degrees, each major 'promise' is triggered by an undertaking.

As Worshipful Master, you will have to learn the Obligation as an integral part of the Ceremony, and then break it into small chunks so that the Candidate can follow it and repeat each phrase. Here are some examples of the 'trigger phrases' in the Obligations;

- I likewise solemnly promise…

- I further solemnly promise…

- I likewise solemnly engage…

- I further solemnly pledge myself…

So, how to memorise the ones you need for each specific Ceremony? Well, first there is the word 'solemnly' which is common to all of these trigger phrases.

Next comes the use of acronyms.

When you come across a small phrase that troubles your memory, it is a useful trick to replace it mentally with an acronym which means something to you personally, and which is then much simpler to recall and position in sequence.

Everyone has a different library of acronyms to call upon, and it works best if you can choose acronyms that are familiar to you.

My own examples, in the Third Degree, are

- I Likewise Solemnly Engage… = LSE = London School of Economics

- I Further Solemnly Pledge myself = FSP = File Service Protocol

It's irrelevant to the lesson why these specific acronyms Work for me, however they are familiar terms and I found them useful (still do) when dealing with this Ritual, both in terms of remembering the trigger phrases and also the order the they come in. The order is simply remembered because 'Likewise' stands still, then 'Further' moves on.

As you're probably some distance from the Chair at this stage, here are some others you may find useful in the earlier Work

- First Degree Charge; Secrecy, Fidelity and Obedience = SFO = Serious Fraud Office

- First Tracing Board (inter alia); Wisdom, Strength
  & Beauty = WSB = World Series Baseball

Many competent Ritualists I have met use this technique, but like all the other tips and tricks in this Book, you need to find the ones that work for you. If you'd like to try the Acronym method for yourself, there's a really good web resource at www.acronymfinder.com

## Testing Yourself

By now, you should be achieving about 95% accuracy and you shouldn't be hitting any road-blocks when you recite the whole Ceremony. Next you will spend a little time immersed in checking your precision, which will enable you to clear up any outstanding glitches.

So, let's go back to the beginning. Carrying the Book and reading it on the bus might be one way of getting you there, but it's probably not the best way. We need a more sophisticated approach.

## Marking Your Ritual Book

Your first Ritual Book is part of your Masonic time capsule. It was probably given to you by your Proposer into Masonry, and it may have sentimental or nostalgic value for you. It's only a book, and there are thousands like it, but this particular copy may be special to you. If you would prefer to preserve it unsullied, you should.

I which case I suggest you buy another one, as your 'Working Book'. You can mark-up parts of the Work, maybe by underlining passages, or even in different highlight colours to help you learn and re-learn them each time you need to. When I was a Deacon, I found it really helpful to highlight all my own words and perambulations in my Working Book (pink for JD, then yellow for SD), so that I could skip through the whole Ceremony and just concentrate on my parts, by quickly identifying the cues for me to begin and end.

I really recommend you do this, and also annotate other parts where you find it useful to be able to directly draw your attention without wading through pages that aren't relevant to you.

## Mastering Perambulations

A good example is the Senior Deacon's Work in the Raising Ceremony, where it might be useful to number each of the three 'tours' of the Lodge that you will make with the Candidate before the Obligation. Then you can learn and practice each 'Circuit' as a whole piece. Once you have the three different circuits matched to their respective sequence of words and actions, you simply put them back together and they stop being mysterious, they just become Circuits 1, 2, and 3. With a little practice at LoI, you will look slick and confident when you do the floor Work in the Lodge.

## Typing

Typing or Copying sections of the Ritual can be a grey area. Of course the Obligation in your initiation Ceremony exhorts you never to "write those secrets, indict, carve, mark, engrave, or otherwise them delineate". Received wisdom is that the Secrets are, in conventional Working, any words, names or phrases which are abbreviated or blanked out in the Ritual Book. This is logical, I think you'd agree, since any ordinary member of the public can walk into a regalia shop and buy a Ritual Book off-the-shelf without any need to identify themselves as a Freemason. Likewise, most of the Ceremonies can be easily found on the Internet, and often such postings do not even conform to the convention of protecting the Secrets.

## Copyright

Of course there is the Law of Copyright, which is there to protect the owner of the printed material from people ripping it off and illegitimately profiting from it. As an author myself, I am wholly supportive of this important law, because without it the entire creative community (writers, artists, musicians, and so on) would starve! The law is clear; you cannot copy protected Work, and that includes both written and recorded copying.

However, there is a facility in copyright law called "Fair Use", which allows for the limited use of copies for specific non-commercial applications. According to the Copyright Service in the UK, this allows for "research and private study" without infringing copyright.

A mainstream example is the use of textbooks in schools, where it is quite normal for students to write or type verbatim passages in their course work. You might reasonably interpret this as allowing you to re-type a passage of Ritual and use it for your own private study, as long as you do not make it available to anyone else, by any means. I would also suggest that this practice would only be reasonable provided that you had purchased a legitimate version of the original Work in the first place, i.e. you bought a Ritual Book, so that the author and publisher have lost nothing in the process.

If you are in any doubt about your rights and responsibilities regarding copyright, I would refer you to www.copyrightservice.co.uk, the authority site on such matters in the UK.

Typing has a multiplying effect on the learning process, because it forces you to read and interpret, and to memorise for the short-term. There's a strong communications channel between your eyes and your hands, and information passes through several processes from you reading it to actually pressing the correct keys to type it out. You will certainly be using your memory to store the little pieces of information whilst you put them through the various stages of conversion from a visual image to a set of complex actions, and these small memories are absorbed into your overall knowledge of the piece.

Next, as you type there is a further inception process going on in your brain. This time your eyes are reading, and your brain is auditing the correctness of your typing, so again you are interpreting the image and giving it a 'pass/fail' check against your original memory.

Typing into a PC also gives you numerous advantages in terms of the portability and versatility of the 'script'. Once you have an electronic version, you can do other things with it to help you learn, as long as you stay within the copyright law. Obviously you can print out sections on small pages and carry them in your pocket or in your wallet, which gives you multiple opportunities to check the Work whilst you are learning it, without having to carry a Ritual Book with you.

Additionally, most WP software allows you to create documents in different formats, different page sizes, and different font sizes. One of the most useful facilities, to be found in virtually all modern programs, is the ability to store a document as a 'portable document format' PDF file, which can then be read in Adobe Acrobat as well as a host of other third-party programs. The greatest advantage of PDF files is that they can be side-loaded onto smart phones, tablets, and E-readers such as the Amazon Kindle. So now you have your Ritual Book on virtually any device. PDF files on your smart phone enable you to learn Ritual passages on the bus or the train without it looking as though you're on your way to a Bible class!

At the time of writing, most Ritual Societies and Publishers have not made the 'Books' available on the Kindle store. Sales of electronic Books are now overhauling physical printed copies in many categories. During a recent quick check, I found the Bristol Craft Workings and the Royal Arch Ritual on Amazon, so hopefully it won't be long before the others follow suit, which will avoid the need for DIY solutions!

If you decide to use this method, there are a few things that are worth knowing which will save you some time. First of all, when you are typing into your PC it's best to use a small page size setup, such as A6. It's more suitable for the size of the screen that you are going to be using. Secondly, choose a font size which is going to be readable on your smart-phone: A minimum 14 or 16 point size is fine, and you should try to use a serifated font such as Times New Roman, which is generally easier to read in blocks of text.

Finally, set up the margins as 'narrow', and this will, in conjunction with the other two points, give you a readable display on the small screen.

If it is not your intention to use a tablet, Kindle, or smart phone in this way, it is still useful to set up your typed document so that, for example, you create four "panels" of text on an A4 printed sheet, so that you can fold it into quarters which will slip neatly into your wallet or pocket. Use the 'columns' function and move the paragraphs around until you get a nice position for the folds in the paper.

**Comparison Checking**

Another useful software tool is that you can self-check your understanding and memorisation. Many Word Processing apps give you the ability to Compare Documents side-by-side, a practice often used by lawyers when checking contracts (known as Legal Blackline). To do this, you will first need to create a "Master" document, which is a correct facsimile of the Ritual you are learning. Put that aside, and when you are ready to practice your recital, create a new blank document and re--type the passage from memory. Once you have done this you can use the "Compare Documents" function in Word which will show you the variations (i.e. your mistakes) inside the master document.

If you have followed the recommendations earlier in the Book, particularly in terms of cramming the "big-picture" early in the process, then this method will help you to refine your precision, and if you repeat it regularly you will clearly see the progress you are making in eliminating grammatical errors and syntax mistakes.

Nobody expects you to be perfect, however there's nothing stopping you from trying!

An excellent Application for smart phones and tablets is PDF Reader, which costs £1.99 on the Apple App Store at time of writing. It has some great features, such as the ability to receive documents as e-mails and then store them in custom folders on your phone or tablet. Indeed, Adobe themselves now have an Adobe Reader Application which can be downloaded for free on both Apple and Android devices.

But remember; do not make copies of any part of the Ritual available to anyone else or place them in the public domain.

### So, What If You Don't Type?

All of the above methods work perfectly well with handwriting, but of course it is difficult to carry handwriting onto an electronic device. Nevertheless, writing and re-writing the Ritual longhand is a perfectly valid method of memorising the Work.

Index cards or Post-It notes can do the job if you prefer handwriting.

### The Naughty Schoolboy Method

I don't know if they still enforce this kind of punishment in school, but when I was a kid, a well-known and hated penalty for misbehaviour was the "100 Lines". I'm sure you know about this, because it's such a cliché, but in case you don't, it goes like this;

If you were caught (for example) copying someone else's work, you might be ordered by your teacher to "write a hundred lines". The line would typically be something like...

"I must not copy other people's Work"

...which you would be compelled to write long-hand, usually during a detention period, then present to the teacher and your punishment would be discharged. In the case of particularly vindictive teachers, or particularly heinous offences, the lines might have to be written in chalk on the blackboard (another historical curiosity). Whatever the case, a by-product of the punishment was that the particular sentence, after a hundred repetitions, was so well ingrained into your consciousness (and subconsciousness) that it would stay there for a long, long time. Whether it actually had any beneficial effect on your dreadful behaviour is debatable!

It is definitely low-tech, but the same principle can be used to learn particularly troublesome short passages, and quickly.

I first experimented with this the first time I tried to learn the Royal Arch Mystical Lecture, which you may have heard. The whole lecture is quite complicated, but there is a particularly irksome paragraph concerning 'The Name on the Circle' which is horrible to memorize. Having struggled with it for days, I broke it down into its five natural sections, each a long sentence, and over a period of five days I used the 'writing lines' method in order to memorise each sequence of words. I discovered that the optimum exercise was to write each line twenty times, and to repeat the exercise three times a day, first thing in the morning, sometime in the afternoon, and once in the evening just before bed. It's about five minutes each time, and it's a great excuse to buy one of those elegant Moleskine notebooks that people from Advertising Agencies carry around.

The beauty of the Naughty Schoolboy method, which is, I repeat, only really practical for those particularly troublesome short passages, is that you don't actually have to tax your memory at all. You can copy the first line directly from the Book if you want, and then copy each subsequent line from the one above. All you do is spend a few minutes copying and writing, and your marvellous subconscious memory does the rest for you.

It really Works! As for its applicability in Craft Ritual, it's a pretty good way to learn those tricky little lists of 'attributes' that crop up regularly (the Lists), for example;

- The Four Cardinal Virtues (First Tracing Board); Temperance, Fortitude, Prudence and Justice

- The Seven Liberal Arts And Sciences (in the Second Tracing Board); Grammar, Rhetoric, Logic, Arithmetic, Geometry, Music, Astronomy

- The Five Noble Orders Of Architecture; Tuscan, Doric, Ionic, Corinthian and Composite

**Rhythm and Metering**

It appears that the popular English Constitution Ritual variants are all descended from more or less a single source, which seems to be the Emulation Lodge of Improvement, which was originally formed in 1823 and still Works weekly to this day, in London.

Whatever its origins, there's no doubt that the Craft Ritual is exquisitely constructed, and packed full of patterns and rhythms which, if you train yourself to recognise them, can be very useful in helping you to memorise and perform the Ceremonies well. It would also be true to say that some of the language is arguably clumsy and does not flow at all well, but there are highlights throughout every Ceremony which, if you identify and learn them properly, can be used as 'anchors', those safe landing points which are spaced throughout the Ceremonies as places of familiarity and comfort.

A really fine example of rhythmic Ritual, almost a song in itself, is this passage in our example, the Charge After Passing (Taylors);

> Your past behaviour
> and regular deportment
> have merited the honour
> which we have conferred,
> and in your new character
> it is expected,
> that you will not only conform
> to the principles of the order
> but will steadily persevere with
> the practice of every virtue.

If that doesn't speak to you at first, try tapping your foot along to an imaginary beat whilst you read it out loud, and you'll soon get it. Imagine each line is a musical bar, and has two beats

The Craft Ritual is full of examples of rhythm and metering that you'll find can be applied to help with learning. It's not a magic bullet, but it is another tool which you can add to your box of tricks that make it easier to remember those tricky passages.

Here are two other shorter examples of well-constructed and rhythmic language;

- Judge with candour, admonish with friendship, reprehend with mercy

- Wisdom to contrive, strength to support, beauty to adorn

When you first read the Ritual passage aloud to yourself,

you might immediately start to spot these little 'rhythm sections'. You can mark them with a highlight pen as you discover them, and they may quickly become the parts you learn first that hang the whole thing together for you.

## Starting To Rehearse

In this Chapter we have cemented some techniques to get you through Stage Two by focusing on memorising, checking and reciting the authentic version of the Work you're learning. Now we need to think about transitioning to Stage Three, the Rehearsal phase. It's important that you confirm to yourself that the Work is now solidly implanted into your memory.

You shouldn't really start rehearsing the delivery until you've mastered the text. If you have followed the instructions so far, you should be well on the way by now.

## Chapter 5 Summary

- In Stage Two, the objective is to Polish your Work until it is accurate and automatic

- Maintain your Practice Schedule using the same Alarm techniques as Stage One

- The Morning and Bed-Time routines are very valuable

- Identify Lists and Sequences and learn them separately

- Practice Visualisation to help with Perambulations

- Use repetition to identify and correct small 'link word' errors

- Use familiar acronyms and abbreviations to remember tricky phrases

- Mark-up your Ritual Book. Buy a second one if necessary

- Use diagrams to understand and de-mystify sections of Perambulations

- Use your Smartphone, Tablet or E-Reader so you always have your Work available

- Look for rhythmic language to help you develop your knowledge of the Work

# 6
# LODGE OF INSTRUCTION

If you're really serious about Ritual, even if you only want to do one Ceremony to establish yourself in the Lodge, it is impossible to understate the importance of Lodge of Instruction.

LoI comes in many forms. Many Lodges have a dedicated LoI that meets every week. Some of these are well organised, well planned and well-structured affairs that take the Ritual very seriously and endeavour to produce excellent renditions of the Ceremonies.

Some are less systematic in their approach, perhaps with one eye on some beer drinking. Nevertheless, these LoI's actually deliver a pretty good result, because they do, by virtue of their inherently sociable environment, tend to attract regular attendance!

Most will fall somewhere between the two. Whatever the case, the LoI is a critical element for a Brother who is working his way through the various Offices. You can be certain that a Mason who does not regularly attend LoI will definitely struggle when (and if) he reaches the Chair which is a shame because your Masters Year is the pinnacle of your Craft Masonry career. It should be an enjoyable experience for you, but more particularly it should be a pleasure for the other Brethren.

So even if Ritual is not your main mission in life (and it needn't be) if you are serious about becoming Master of your Lodge you should really make an effort to attend LoI regularly, starting as early as you can.

LoI can be a lot of fun once you get used to it because Masons are usually a welcoming bunch. There are many Lodges where attendance at LoI is mandatory if you want to be considered for progress through the Offices. This is fine if your Lodge is well-subscribed and there is competition for offices. In this case, you really have no option but to fall in line and attend regularly; otherwise you may either be systematically overlooked, or just forgotten about. Out of sight, out of mind, as the saying goes.

## How to Get Offered the Work You Want

There's plenty of variation in the ways that Lodges 'allocate' the work to their Officers and Brethren. Most Lodges have a 'Standing Committee' or 'General Purposes Committee' which meets a few weeks before each Regular Lodge Meeting in order to plan the proceedings. If you intend to make your way as an active Ritualist in your Lodge, it is well worthwhile to attend the Committee meetings if you're allowed within your Lodge By-Laws. The allocation of the work may be decided autonomously by the Master, maybe under advisement from the Secretary, and where there is a strong and active Lodge of Instruction, the Preceptor will undoubtedly contribute his advice as to who amongst the Brethren is potentially equipped to participate in different parts of the Ceremony.

The problem seems to be that often these committees only meet a month or so ahead of the meeting, and that really doesn't allow enough time for you to learn a Ceremony from a standing start. This is perhaps one reason why the same familiar faces pop up in many Lodges, especially when it comes to Charges and Tracing Boards, because a month may only be enough time for someone to revise a large Ceremony they have learned before.

So, you have to find a way to get more warning. My recommendation is that you approach the Preceptor of your Lodge of Instruction, and seek out his advice You might perhaps tell him that you've been thinking about a Ceremony that you would like to try at a *future* Lodge meeting, and ask him to advise you on whether it should be Ceremony A or Ceremony B?

Think about the work that your Lodge will perform over the coming, say, six to nine months. What is the succession of Candidates coming through? Can you see, for example, a Second Degree Ceremony about four to six months away?

For the purpose of this example, let's assume that you are not serving in one of the Working Offices, particularly Deacons, as this would mean you already have enough work to do!

Pick something. For a Passing, there are three choices; The Working Tools, which many Masons consider to be a very special Ceremony, the Charge After Passing, which I consider to be one of the best constructed pieces of Masonic Ritual, and the Tracing Board, which in and of itself is a major challenge, even more so when you add in the extended section from Emulation or West End Working.

You will recall that we chose the Charge After Passing as probably the easiest to learn and memorise, plus it has no perambulations or demonstrations involved. It would be a good choice for the novice Ritualist.

## Can't Make It To Lodge Of Instruction?

If you find that you have joined a Lodge whose LoI schedule conflicts with your other responsibilities, it may be practical for you to find another LoI nearby which fits better with your work or family life. This is not at all unusual. You will be welcomed as a Brother, and if you clearly communicate the situation to the Preceptor of your own LoI, it will usually work out OK.

The ideal LoI is often like a little club, perhaps meeting in a side room at the Masonic Centre, or in the back room of a pub (where some say Masonry originated!) I'm going to assume that your Lodge has a Lodge of Instruction, or shares one with other Lodges in the locality, so you already know how things work. Instead, it makes more sense to focus on how to get the best out of LoI, because it is by far the best (and maybe the only) opportunity to boost your Ritual performance in the company of your peers.

## LoI Officers

The boss of the LoI is called the Preceptor, and is usually (and hopefully) an experienced Past Master who is well versed in all the Craft Ritual. The Preceptor is usually elected each year, and a good Preceptor may have held the office for a number of years. Some LoI's also elect Deputy Preceptors, who are there to stand-in when the Preceptor is absent. There will usually be a Secretary, who will take minutes and attend to the administrative business of the LoI, just like a real Lodge. There may also be a Treasurer and even a Charity Steward in some larger LoI's.

LoI is not for learning Ritual prose; hopefully you have understood that if you have followed the instructions thus far, you need to do this on your own or privately with help from other Brethren. You go to LoI to practice.

The conventional functions which a Lodge of Instruction delivers are these.

- Perambulations; LoI provides the only realistic environment for you to practice the 'walking about' parts of the Ceremony. In fact, the first time you attempt a Ceremony (probably as a Deacon) which requires perambulations, the Ritual Book will probably not be much help to you. Although the Book does give reasonably precise instructions on the perambulations, unless you are very familiar with the layout of the Temple, it's unlikely that you will be able to memorize these important movements from text alone.

- Passwords and Salutes; These are not written out in the Ritual book, but are passed down by verbal or demonstration means, so the only places you will see and hear them are in the Lodge itself, or in the LoI. You can ask a more experienced Brother to give you the passwords you might need to learn for a specific Ceremony, but of course you are bound by your Obligations to keep them secret and not write them down, so LoI is really the only place to become familiar with these important words and actions.

- Sequence; How the whole Ceremony fits together, and then fits into the context of the overall meeting. By attending LoI you will get to observe the mechanics of how the Lodge works through the Summons, going up and down through the Degrees. Familiarity with the sequences will be a great help to your confidence in the Lodge itself.

- Questions; At LoI, whilst there are protocols to be observed (it should be run like a proper Lodge Meeting) it is always possible to approach any other Brother with questions you might struggle to ask in the formal setting of the Lodge itself. Even the most senior Freemason will have time for you at LoI, and you can learn a lot of valuable stuff.

Some Lodges of Instruction hold what are called 'Officers

Nights' in the last few weeks before the Meeting proper. The idea of an Officers Night is that all the Officers, and anyone else who is taking part in the Ceremonies at the forthcoming meeting, can come to the LoI and have a complete rehearsal of the whole Meeting. Sometimes it is the only opportunity to work with the other Officers, because not everyone can get to LoI regularly.

If you are participating in a Ceremony, you must make every effort to attend at least one Officers Night at your LoI so that you are comfortable with your part and role, and everyone trusts you.

## Floorwork Homework

If you have a Deacon's job to do and you need to practice the Ceremony including the perambulations but you cannot make it to LoI regularly, find a way to rehearse at home or in a room somewhere private.

By now you should understand the layout of the Lodge, with the WM in the E, the JW in the S, the SW in the W, and the Secretary's Table in the North. Nominate some bits of furniture to be those positions, and walk and talk the Ceremony around the room. Once you have gone through it a couple of times, you should easily be able to remember where you need to go at each stage, whilst you can practice the words and the salutes as well. You can easily do this on your own, and it will allow you to hit the ground running each time you go to LoI.

By all means, use the drawings or diagrams we explored earlier to help you remember the floor work.

## The Initiation Ceremony at LoI

I mentioned in an earlier Chapter that if you are serious about eventually taking the Chair of your Lodge, it would be very useful to have some experience of the Masters Work before you get there, because it's a lot to take in if you leave it all until your Master's Year.

Lodge of Instruction should, in the preceding years, be able to accommodate you. The most important thing is to explain to the Preceptor and the other Members what you are trying to do, which is to prepare for a year as Master of the Lodge (should it be forthcoming). Many LoI's positively encourage this kind of speculative practice work during off-peak times, when the pressure is not on their Officers to rehearse for a forthcoming Ceremony.

I recommend that you aim to try the Initiation Ceremony from the Chair well before you will need to perform it. It's probably the most important Ceremony that the Lodge performs, and certainly it's important for the Candidate coming in, so it's a good plan to follow.

Suggest to your Preceptor that you'd like to try the various sections in parts, so you can take it at a steady pace and slot in the practice when the LoI Masters Chair is available from time to time. Usually the experienced Brethren will be very pleased to have someone who is enthusiastic to try new things, whom they can mentor and coach along the way.

Don't wait for this, because in the lead up to your Installation as Master, the LoI will be fully focused on the Installation Ceremony. You need to take the Initiation Ceremony with you into the Chair, not learn it once you get there.

## Learning Degree Ceremonies for the Chair

Nowhere is it more true that 'time is of the essence' than the first time you learn a Degree Ceremony. Don't worry though; once you've done the First Degree, the Second is not so arduous. The Third Degree needs a book of its own!

Degree Ceremonies lend themselves best to be learned out of sequence. So, the system for you to learn the Initiation Ceremony, using all the strategies and techniques explained in this book, is as follows;

- Learn the big monologues first. These form around 75% of the Ceremony, but once you have them, you have your 'anchors' and it's much easier to learn the other parts.

  o Obligation

  o Exhortation

  o Explanation of the Secrets

  o Charge

- Next, learn the Working Tools (unless you are delegating it)

  o It really helps to have a set, if not just draw them on pieces of card. You can add some prompts on the cards for use in the memorisation process, but you should discard the prompts as soon as you are close to remembering them.

- Next, learn the Questions to the Candidate (the beginning of the Initiation Ceremony) and the preamble that leads up to the Obligation. For the questions, a numbering system is advised.

- Next, learn Presentation of the Badge (Apron). It's a short, important piece that often gets overlooked until the last minute!

- Now you have 90% of the work under your belt. The remaining parts will need LoI;

  o Admission of the Candidate

  o Re-Admission of the Candidate

  o All the other short links between these parts

**Performance Practice**

When you are learning and preparing one of the

Monologues, or Lectures, for example The Working Tools, Charges, or Tracing Board Lectures, you will do most of the learning work alone. If you have followed the recommendations and systems in the earlier Chapters, you should have mastered memorizing your work, and should now be quite comfortable speaking the Work out loud (as long as nobody's around to listen!).

But in order to start to prepare for the performance itself, it's important that you find opportunities to practice your 'recital' in something approaching the context of a real Lodge Meeting, and that is where LoI is particularly useful.

You will be encouraged to perform your work as an integral part of the Ceremony being rehearsed in LoI, so you will not only get to try out the performance aspect, but also you will get used to the way your part fits into the whole. Details like where you will be sitting before the DC collects you, where you will stand for your performance, and what happens afterwards, will all improve your confidence on the day and help you to ensure that your participation is smooth and seamless.

## Posture And Delivery

People will only notice if you are awkward or unconventional. If you seem comfortable, they will feel comfortable too.

So in the early days of your career as a Ritualist, it makes more sense to worry less about the fine details of posture and delivery, and make the process as simple as possible.

- Stand up straight, but natural, and try to relax your body.

- Speak clearly, at a moderate speed. Keep breathing, pause often.

- If it helps, wave your hands around, but not too much!

These three elements can be your basic 'rules'. If you can

stick to them, you will accomplish the mission. Later on, you can add nuance and gesture, if you feel so inclined, but for now all that matters is that people notice you because of the Ritual you deliver.

So, work on finding a natural relaxed stance at LoI, and at home when you rehearse. Tension in the shoulders is a manifestation of stress; likewise if you forcefully relax your shoulders, the stress will dissipate, so practice like this;

- Stand up straight, whatever that means to you.

- Close your eyes for a moment

- Focus your attention on the muscles in your shoulders and neck

- Inhale deeply, and then exhale slowly, whilst you...

- Push out the tension and let your shoulders drop (don't hunch forwards)

- Open your eyes and notice how relaxed you have become in just a few seconds.

Once you have tried it a few times, start practicing without closing your eyes. Before long you will find that you can relax really easily and virtually on-demand.

For your information, this is part of the basic method behind self-hypnosis.

**Pronunciation and Projection**

The simple instruction here is that people need to be able to hear you and understand what you are saying. So there are two things you need to practice;

- Pronouncing the words correctly

- Speaking clearly

Maybe you already speak like a BBC newsreader, or perhaps you have a broad regional accent (which may be from somewhere else in the country). Perhaps you have a foreign accent, or a speech impediment. Whatever the case, you owe it to your audience to do your best to deliver well-spoken Ritual. You shouldn't be thinking about changing the way you speak, or trying to be someone you're not, but this is 'Presentation-Speak' and everyone can do it. It's that slightly 'posher' version of your own voice that you might use, say, if the Queen came round for tea one day! It's your 'Telephone Voice'. It's your 'Interview Voice'

As far as clear speech is concerned, you need to work this out based on the best you can be whilst still feeling relatively relaxed whilst speaking. The biggest challenge to clear speech, or more particularly the fluency of it, is poor recall. If you are struggling to remember what to say next you have not put enough attention into the early memorization task. This programme is tailored towards a fixed chronological timetable, which requires you to complete the three stages sequentially and completely. When you do this, you are able to recite the Ceremony naturally and fluently, which is the core of a confident performance.

Here is a good definition of Confidence; 'Competence Delivered'.

### Performance Pressure

You may also discover the first couple of times that you perform your work before an LoI audience, that although you were word-perfect in the shower that morning, it's a different story altogether when you do it for real.

This may be your first taste of 'Performance Pressure', sometimes termed 'Choking' and it can be very frustrating. Knowing something doesn't necessarily mean a person will remember it properly when faced with the presence of an audience and the need to do a good job.

So the first step in overcoming the tendency to Choke is to

simulate the performance situation and re-run the exercise as many times as possible, and the only place where this is really viable is in the Lodge of Instruction.

It's really important to push (respectfully) to get your opportunities. The more rehearsals you can achieve in the weeks preceding the actual Meeting, the better prepared you will be the first time you stand up to Work in Open Lodge Assembled.

It's not such a problem if you're preparing Officers work, such as Inner Guard or Junior Deacon, because you'll be under some pressure to attend LoI in order to fit into the general rehearsal of the Degree Ceremonies. But if you are performing a Lecture, as we discussed earlier, you will need to elbow your way to the front from time to time, in order to get enough live practice time in LoI. The LoI doesn't really need to hear you, but you need to try it in front of an audience.

Don't be shy. Just find your allies, be ready, and take it on.

Your Lodge of Instruction is a Masonic Lodge in all but the most formal sense. It is specifically designed to provide instruction and practise in the Ritual. You should use it as such, because the first time you are able to deliver your Ritual to an acceptable standard at LoI, you will know that you are ready to do exactly the same thing in the Temple. Your LoI audience is likely to be a lot more critical than the Lodge Meeting itself, so if you can do it there, you can do it anywhere!

## Chapter 6 Summary

- Try to immerse yourself in Lodge Of Instruction; it will pay big dividends.

- Attend Standing Committee to get the 'inside track' on forthcoming Work.

- If your own LoI is inconvenient, join one nearby that works for you.

- Rehearse the perambulations at home, and then practice them at LoI with the team.

- Be ambitious, especially if you are getting closer to the Chair.

- Use LoI to understand the pattern and sequence of the whole Ceremony.

- Don't get hung up on Posture; find a comfortable relaxed style that works for you.

- Teach yourself to Relax on-demand.

- Develop your 'Telephone Voice' to speak clearly and enunciate.

- Remember; "Confidence is Competence Delivered"

# 7
# STAGE THREE: REHEARSAL

Let's briefly re-cap where you are; So far, we've been following a sequence which should have gone like this;

- Observation; you visited a Lodge to see 'your' Work being performed in a real situation, to get a feel for the context, and to "Measure The Work".

- Planning; You broke down your work into daily portions. You counted them, and used the 2:1:1 ratio to calculate your timetable.

- Cramming (Memorising); you used all the techniques and short-cuts, finding out which ones worked for you, and you 'Crammed' the Work into your memory. You established your daily practice routines.

- Polishing; You then employed another set of techniques and strategies to iron out all the kinks and to get as close as possible to a perfect rendition of your Work.

- Lodge Of Instruction; hopefully you'll have had the chance to try out your Work in LoI, and you'll have a good feel for how close you are to being able to deliver it for real.

By now, you should be around three-quarters of the way through your timetable for the allotted Work. The final phase of this learning exercise is to work on the Performance aspects.

## Repetition

I hope that you are still following the systems you learned in the first phase, to continue to mentally and verbally recite your Work at every opportunity. The more of this simple practice you do, the less you risk forgetting a word or drying up when it comes to the big day.

As you practice, you will notice the improvements yourself. At first, having broken the passage into sections, you had to think about how to move from the end of one section to the start of the next, and what order the sentences came in. By now, you should have virtually eliminated that conscious effort, and you should be moving seamlessly from one section to the next, so that the parts have become a whole.

Even now, it's important to continue to check yourself against the Book, perhaps using one of the techniques we explored in Stage Two, to ensure that you haven't picked up any bad habits. When you're rehearsing in LoI, unless you are very specific, or the Preceptor is an absolute stickler, you may pass over small mistakes such as single words or re-arranged phrases without anyone pulling you up on it. So it's important to keep checking the veracity of your own memory. You have all the tools, so use them.

If you are learning a Lecture, you may only need to take a look at the Book every few days, or if a small question about accuracy arises in your own mind (this happens).

If you are learning Work which involves perambulations, usually a Degree Ceremony, then the way to use the book is to cover the page with something like a business card, which you can slide down as you work your way through the Ceremony. This allows you to read and understand the flow of the Ceremony itself, identifying the cues for you to do or say something, then rehearse your part before you uncover that particular part of the page. You should always be testing yourself.

This repetitious recital, whether it's silent or spoken, simply drives the prose deeper into your subconscious, where it will remain, in some form, more or less forever. This is what you are trying to achieve, because although the primary intention of this book is to get you through your first Ritual performance, an important by-product is that once you earn a Ceremony for the first time, if you do it right, it will be there for you to revise and deliver again in the future with much less work. One day, you could be Preceptor of your LoI.

It's also important, as we previously discussed, that you perform the WHOLE piece as often as possible, in order to balance your familiarity with the later portion against the earlier portion, which you learned first.

## Serious Rehearsal

Let's make the assumption that you still have some time to go before the Big Day, and that you've tried at least one full run through of your Work in the LoI. If that went well, just keep doing what you're doing and you'll be fine.

Some people will have discovered a lot about themselves at LoI, and you may be apprehensive about how you are going to get yourself ready to do it for real. This is where the Ritualists separate themselves from the crowd, because they know that the Performance aspect is where the real Work is done.

You need to Seriously Rehearse, and you need to do it at least once (probably twice) every single day in the lead up to the Meeting.

The simplest recommendation here is that you need to shut yourself away with no distractions, and deliver your Work out loud and completely. Find somewhere private, which may be as simple as closing your office door at lunchtime, or, as a farmer Brother told me he likes to do, go and stand in the milking shed at six o'clock in the morning and deliver the Ritual to the herd!

Rehearsing is no more complicated than practicing an instrument, if you play one, or having a telephone conversation with your wife or girlfriend. If you are a traveler, hotel rooms are perfect because they are usually soundproof, you are usually alone, and you will usually have time to spare.

The critical point is that you are not just reciting, you are Rehearsing. You need to stand up, exactly as you will be in the Lodge, and you need to speak at normal volume, exactly as you will need to do on the day. You may find that once you start to put a little effort into the diction and delivery, you'll suddenly discover a few small places where your memorisation may be weak. This is a great opportunity to address those, and you will be able to fix them really quickly.

The key benefit of this rehearsal style, apart from practicing the monologue, is that you will start to use your aural sense (of the ear) which will open a new channel into your memory. You will start to train yourself how the Ritual sounds to you when you are performing it, and this will enable you to more truly appreciate the rhythms and patterns in the language which might have eluded you in the earlier phases.

When you rehearse the Ritual out-loud, you are multiplying the effectiveness over a silent recital. So do it as often as you can, and be as authentic as possible.

A couple of points;

Firstly, I have heard of people using a mirror to aid rehearsal. Frankly, it may work for some people, but I can't really see the point.

In the Rehearsal phase, you are trying to internalise the processes of memory recall, to focus your senses on the main skills needed to retain and repeat a complex sequence of language. Watching yourself do this seems an unnatural situation and a potential distraction from the focus you are trying to achieve. There won't be a mirror in the Lodge, and the objective here is to try to replicate as closely as possible the real situation that you will be in.

Secondly, although I eschew the use of audio recording as a primary learning tool, in the rehearsal phase it can be very useful as a method of self-critique.

You don't need a separate recorder (our Ancient Brethren called it a Dictaphone). Most smart-phones are equipped with a high quality voice recorder, so use it if you think it will help.

Do it like this;

1. Rehearse the passage once or twice, out loud, to the best of your ability. Get into the mind-set that you are preparing to record it, so that you are building up to a peak.

2. Set up your phone (or other recording device) so that you don't have to hold it.

3. When you feel ready, start the Voice Recorder and deliver the Work. In the beginning it's OK to break it into sections if it's a big piece like a Degree Ceremony or a Tracing Board. But try to get through each section without pausing. If you make an error, don't dwell on it; just keep moving (because that's the way you want to deal with any mistakes when you do it for real).

4.  Finally, play back the recording, and have your book open whilst you listen, so that you can check yourself for any grammatical errors that might have registered whilst you were reciting it.

5.  Now delete that recording. Repeat the process as many times as you need to. You will probably get bored with the repetition, but that's a good sign because that will indicate that you are ready to move on.

If you are really brave, try video. Again, your phone is good for this.

## Rehearsing with a Partner

On any given evening, lights burn brightly from the windows of garden sheds all over this land...

It's essential to have systems and techniques for learning and rehearsing on your own, however rehearsing with a partner can be really helpful too. I know many Brethren who visit each other's homes in order to rehearse Ritual in front of a friendly audience of one. This is a great idea and I can't recommend it enough. It's not practical for everyone, but you'd be surprised how many people will gladly invite you round to rehearse, if you make it known that that is what you are looking for. And of course there's always a cup of tea or the odd bottle of beer, though I would caution you against attempting to rehearse anything serious whilst sampling another Brother's home-brew!

If you are fortunate enough to have a friend in the Craft who you can rehearse with, make sure you agree to be brutally honest about each other's performances, because you need accurate and timely critique throughout the process.

And it doesn't necessarily have to be done at home. Two Brethren I know who are neighbours but belong to different Lodges walk to the pub together most evenings, and test each other on the way. They carry each other on the way home!

**In The Car**

If you get to spend a lot of time on your own in the car, you have a great opportunity to become really good at Masonic Ritual. You can practice to your heart's content, so don't waste the opportunity.

Boring motorway journeys are the best. As with the earlier learning strategies, it's a good idea to pre-plan your in-car rehearsal time. This stops you procrastinating. You really need to turn off your phone, and turn off the radio too, because even at low volume it will disturb your attention.

Of course you can't read or check the book whilst you are driving, so it lends itself to doing larger run-throughs when you've already learned most of the Ceremony. However, because you can't check the book, it forces you to use memory recall whenever you hit a snag, which will help to sharpen your powers.

Running through the same piece two or three times, although it can be a bit boring, is a really good way to make progress whilst you are driving, and you might be surprised about how much more you remember by the third time than the first time. Remember, Masonic Language is about flow, rhythm and sequence, and these attributes really start to deliver when you are rehearsing out loud.

Earlier, we discussed how rehearsing 'out-loud' has a multiplying effect on your progress. It also has hugely beneficial effects to your confidence.

**Your Targets**

There are many factors which go into a great performance, probably enough to fill another book. For the purpose of this, however there are the three most significant attributes which you should be targeting;

- Competence

- Confidence

- Sincerity

## Competence

if you have followed the systems and processes so far, you will have achieved a level of competence which should enable you to be able to give a basic recital of the Work without serious errors. You may not be totally perfect, but that shouldn't concern you now. If you can get the words out, more or less in the right order, then your competence is established. Masonry being a progressive science, it is only logical that competence should be one of the key underlying attributes of the next (and probably most important) factor.

## Confidence

Remember, Confidence is defined a 'Competence Delivered'.

First and foremost, don't confuse nerves with lack of confidence! There are many Brethren who have decades of Ritual experience under their belts, who still get nervous. However they don't lack confidence because they know that they have the competence to deliver the Ceremony, having done it before.

So it's okay to feel a little bit nervous. I mentioned earlier the commonality between excitement and anxiety. Both of these are physical reactions of the body to the anticipation of what lies ahead. They are not quite the same, but are sufficiently similar as to be virtually interchangeable based on context. In other words, the body and mind react more or less the same way to the anticipation of a pleasant forthcoming event as an unpleasant one, but a person's perception of whether the event is going to be pleasant and positive versus unpleasant and negative has a determining effect on how they feel what they feel. Hence nerves and excitement are versions of the same thing.

So, how is this relevant to confidence?

In a number of talking therapies such as cognitive behavioural therapy (CBT) and some branches of hypnotherapy, a technique known as re-framing is often used to teach the subject how to take control of these physical feelings and alter the underlying context, so that a feeling of anxiety or apprehension may actually be re-framed into one of positive anticipation or even excitement. Of course we don't have time here or the techniques to hand to start messing around in psychology, however just the fact that you now have this knowledge may enable you, if you are of a nervous disposition, to help yourself.

One of the common factors of both anxiety and excitement is that they both act on other systems in the body in order to focus energy and concentration where it is needed. Everyone knows about "fight or flight" which is our ancient genetic response to fear or danger, where a huge blast of stimulating chemicals, particularly adrenaline, surges into the bloodstream in order to enable the body to channel all of its resources and energy towards the faculties that are most important in that threatening situation. Vision, response, hearing and other vital capabilities can become temporarily enhanced, whilst digestion and other non-essential services will be momentarily suspended.

Spider senses tingling!

So a nervous disposition can also work to your advantage. Of course nobody expects you to be frightened for your life when you're going into the Lodge to perform your Ritual! However, if you are able to do so, you can perhaps utilise any nervous anticipation you may be feeling to focus yourself on the really important aspects of the task ahead.

So, let's analyse if you are areas in which confidence is important.

## Will I Remember The Work?

Almost every Ritualist hits a roadblock during a performance at one time or another. Don't be frightened of this; it's no reflection on your ability or your efforts. It just happens. That's why you need to have a good understanding with your prompter. Trying to perform Ritual in the Temple without a prompter is like the flying trapeze without a safety net. You may never need it, but if you get a snag halfway through and there's nothing there to fall back on, or nobody to catch you, it will be messy! The next chapter explains how you should work with your prompter to ensure that your safety net is in place without being intrusive.

## What Happens If I Mess Up Perambulations or Salutes?

Usually nothing! If you make a big mistake which is liable to disrupt the Ceremony, you can be sure that someone nearby will pull you up discreetly. Just make sure that you are listening to what's going on around you if you are doing Deacons Work, because almost every other Brother in the Lodge has been in that Office at one time or another, and some of them will actually remember how to do it right!

Of course it is the Director of Ceremonies' responsibility to ensure that movement around the Lodge is conducted correctly. If you are in a Deacon's Office it's always a good idea to have a strong relationship with the DC. You should let him know before each Ceremony if you have any particular concerns, or are confused about where you should be or what you should be doing. Remember, as we said earlier, Freemasons love to help each other so never be afraid to ask. Because no matter how well drilled you were at LOI, once you step onto the Lodge floor, it's a different dynamic.

One common mistake is saluting in the wrong Degree. It usually seems to happen in the Second or Third Degree, when the first Degree salute is given by mistake. I think it's quite simple to understand: most Lodges operate in the first Degree most of the time, so the Brethren simply don't get the practice of using the other salutes regularly. Sometimes it is mentioned, which is almost unavoidable if it happens during the Lodge Opening or Closing Ceremonies, usually by a Warden. But I've done it myself when preparing to present a Tracing Board Lecture, both in the Second Degree and in the Third Degree! Nobody mentioned it at the time, but it came up later on, and I was fined by the Charity Steward at the Festive Board!

This is a simple lapse of concentration, and there is no magic system to avoid it. However, one question that you should be asking yourself regularly throughout your Work is "what Degree are we in?" If you can get into the habit of doing this, it will help you to avoid these little slips.

As we have discussed many times in this book, it's quite rare to see a perfect Ceremony, so you should not allow these small issues to affect the central plank of your confidence going into the Work.

## Confidence-Building Techniques

If you subscribe to the earlier definition of Confidence as 'Competence Delivered', then you will have understood the importance of building a good performance on solid foundations, by applying time and effort to thoroughly learning the Work. You can eliminate almost all the normal obstacles to faultless execution by simply Knowing Your Stuff.

Another aspect of confidence is our natural concern about how people perceive us.

There are a couple of things you should know: many people who appear to be confident in public are actually quite shy in private. The outward confidence they display is a strategy that they have developed in order to deal with their shyness. The strategy is often based around commitment to a process, in other words they use a rigid framework of commitment for tasks, and by focusing on the task and shutting out distractions they are able to do it well. Consequently they successfully de-link the task from their core personality. You may sometimes see this with actors, who appear to be fantastically confident on-stage or on-screen but when you see them on a TV chat show they are shy, or even gauche.

Many, many people have some element of shyness or insecurity hard-wired into their personalities. However you can utilise this knowledge to your advantage when it comes to performing Ritual. When you step out onto the squared pavement you may also be stepping out of your own comfort zone, so it's important that you have made a commitment to do that. It's a little bit like suspending reality for a short time. You leave any imperfections, shyness, lack of confidence, insecurities, or any other negative traits that you may possess, outside the door of the Lodge. There is no great trick to this, you just need to take yourself to one side, take a couple of deep breaths, and let it out.

## The 'Line of Commitment'

As mentioned earlier, Sports Psychologists use a technique called "Line of Commitment" when they are working with individual sportsmen and women.

Many competitors use visualisation techniques, including the 'Line of Commitment'. It's your own personal 'start line' that puts you firmly in control of the task ahead. You mentally create, and physically cross that line only when you are comfortable that you have martialled all your internal resources to accomplish the task.

Golfers are great exponents of this technique; just watch Tiger or any of the top guys, how they act when they step onto the tee. Everyone knows that the great golfers claim to visualise the shot they want before they hit it for real.

You can often see them also looking at their imaginary Line of Commitment, before they take a breath, step over it, and split the fairway. So that seems to work.

Adapting this technique for our purposes, you should follow a sequence as follows;

- Find somewhere private that you can relax and rehearse.

- To begin, confirm your Competence. Remind yourself that you have *learned* the Ritual to the best of your ability. Of course, we would all like longer to practice, but you got what you were given, and you used it wisely.

- You are familiar with the 'performance environment' (the Temple), based on your visits and observations of the Ceremony being performed.

- For Work with Perambulations; You've done the complete Ceremony at Lodge of Instruction.

- For Lectures, You've successfully done a complete delivery to an audience, even if it is only one person.

If you have stuck to your initial plan and the process in this book, you should be able to tick all those boxes. You 'Know Your Stuff'. This is a given fact.

- The next part of the exercise requires you imagine yourself in the performance environment. You may be able to close your eyes and visualise, or you may be more kinaesthetic and be able to 'feel' how it will be. Whatever your own modality, try to use it to 'get into the zone'.

- See what you see, hear what you hear, feel how you feel, and try to identify any part of you that has concerns or questions.

- In your imagination, draw a white line on the floor in front of your feet, about a meter wide and ten centimetres thick. That is your Line of Commitment.

- The very next step you take will be over that Line, and once you have crossed it, you will have committed to start your performance.

Try it; when you have everything ready to go, Step Over The Line and go straight into your Ritual.

Use this technique regularly in rehearsal, and then take it with you to the Lodge on the day of the Meeting. Never cross your Line of Commitment until you are totally ready.

## Control of the Environment

One of the key attributes of the Performance Environment is that it is controllable, by you. Although there are other people in the Temple, they are all 'trained' to conform to the protocols, which means that, barring any major aberration by another Officer in the Ceremony, nothing unexpected is likely to occur. There will be no surprises.

Allied to this, the majority of your audience is assimilating the Ceremony as a complete event, and is unlikely to be monitoring your personal performance in anything other than a general way. The remaining minority are those who are also involved in the Ceremony with you and they are pre-occupied by whatever their next contribution is going to be, so they are not overly concerned with your performance.

If this is going to be your first real attempt at Ritual, you already have a lot of support in your audience. Everyone will want you to do well, but everyone will also make certain allowances for you first time out, so accept that benevolence, and cut yourself some slack. Fluidity and Sincerity are the most noticeable attributes of a great Ritual performance, so don't get too hung up linguistic accuracy.

You control your environment, you know your stuff, and the audience is on your side. It's all good!

## Sincerity

Have you ever heard it said of someone "He could make the telephone directory sound interesting"?

Sincerity is the quality that will ensure you are never remembered as boring, which was a rule on the first page of this book. Sincerity is defined as "freedom from deceit, hypocrisy, or duplicity; probity in intention or in communicating; earnestness". It basically says that you mean what you say.

Like a suntan, Sincerity can cover a multitude of sins! It's another Secret Weapon for the Ritualist, because Sincerity tends to negate criticism, spoken or unspoken, in your audience. If you come across as sincere, people will be distracted from the technical precision of what you are doing, and will get a nice warm feeling about you and your performance. Not only will the reception of your performance be enhanced, but you stand a much better chance of getting away with any imperfections or ad-libs.

The easiest way to sound and feel sincere when you are delivering Ritual is to use intonation in your voice. Test yourself by extracting a few key sentences from the Ritual, sentences that carry some specific meaning, and rehearse them separately, trying different patterns of intonation to place stress on some words or phrases. Inject slightly longer pauses in some places. Play around with the language until it begins to feel natural to you. Remember, you're still in learning mode, and the sound of your own voice will register and resonate inside, and add layers of texture and colour on top of the basic language you have memorised.

I don't propose that you 'manufacture' sincerity when you're in the rehearsal stage of the Ritual process, but more that you relax yourself into it. You deserve the opportunity to add a little emotion into your performance, because you have worked very hard to get to this point. If you can introduce genuine sincerity, you will enjoy it more, and so will your audience.

## Sanity Check

The key idea behind this book is to provide the novice, aspiring, frustrated, or failed Ritualist with a structured method of learning and delivering an acceptable Ritual performance in the Lodge. The main purpose of encouraging you to take part in the Ritual is to enhance your enjoyment of Masonry and fulfil your potential as a Freemason.

You have completed the Competence part in the early Stages. You know your stuff, so there's nothing for you to be concerned about in that department.

With respect to your Confidence, if you can buy into the principle of 'Competence Delivered', you have a sound basis on which to proceed.

However, for some people, confidence is a bigger issue in their lives, one that can hold them back in terms of career, relationships, fitness and health, and lots of other areas. Freemasonry is an excellent forum in which to build confidence and carry it into your normal life.

Sincerity is something for you to experiment with, finding the style that best fits with your feeling for the Ritual and your desire to express yourself during the performance. It is well worth investing a little time in this area, because it can have a massive effect on how you are perceived as a Ritualist.

Of course, all of these are progressive attributes which will grow and develop as you do more and more Ritual in your Lodge.

## Chapter 7 Summary

- Keep your Daily Routines going. The more you practice, the more competent you'll be.

- Aim for at least one complete rehearsal each day.

- Speak out loud whenever you can. It has a multiplying effect on your fluency.

- Rehearse with a partner whenever possible, but be brutal with each other!

- If you're a Deacon, enlist the help and guidance of the DC.

- Once again, remember; "Confidence is Competence Delivered"

# 8
# THE BIG DAY

## Performance Day

Hopefully you have followed the system in this book, and you should be 'ready to go' well in advance of the day of the Meeting.

Even though you're fully rehearsed, it's human nature to doubt yourself. This is irrational; although you will definitely still be looking to improve your confidence towards a solid performance.

Believe in Yourself. You are Ready.

## Weekday or Saturday?

If you are lucky enough to be a member of a Saturday Lodge, you may have a slight advantage, since you probably don't have to go to work on the day of the Lodge Meeting. That will give you the chance to do at least one proper run through, out loud, and perhaps have someone give you a final check-up. Remember, the Ritual evolves in your brain, as you become more accustomed to it, so you will constantly add expression and intonation to your work as each small section becomes permanently implanted in your long-term memory.

However if that is not an option, for example if you are attending a Lodge meeting on a working day, just stick to the system we've been practising in the run up to the meeting.

If your Work is large, you will have figured out the particular passages that worry you, so practice those, and only those, in the bathroom, in the car, on the train, or wherever you do your private rehearsal. Remember the point of this now is to reinforce your powers of recall. So don't worry if you are still stumbling over a few words, just keep going over your suspect passages, working them down one by one until you are relaxed, or as close as you are likely to be!

Whatever your situation, you need to find an opportunity for one complete run-through before you go into the Lodge. This is no longer about you improving your performance; it is all about you demonstrating to yourself exactly how competent you are, so that you can add that knowledge to your confidence. This final run-through can often be the most important step in finally fixing any niggling problems you have, because you know it's the last time you'll rehearse, so you tend to focus on what's really important. You won't get another chance to fix anything, if you don't know it by now, you'll be completely at the mercy of your recall and your Prompter once you 'step off with your left foot'.

### Set Yourself a Deadline

Today, you need to set a cut-off point for yourself. The deal you make with yourself is this; once you pass this point, you will not attempt to change anything about your performance. That's not to say that you can't carry on practising in your head, or even out loud if you can find the opportunity. But at your cut-off point, you have done all the learning you can do, and the version of the Work that you have at that moment is the version you are going to use.

If you are feeling very confident, you might decide that your cut-off point will be as soon as you leave the house to go to the Meeting. At the other end of the scale you may choose your entrance into the Lodge as your cut-off point. It doesn't really matter, so long as you set your deadline and stick to it.

When you get there (maybe you can set another of those pesky vibrating alarms in your phone) you should momentarily stop whatever you are doing, take a breath, and do the relaxation exercise you learned earlier. In that moment, all the learning, the memorizing, and the rehearsing is consigned to your archive, and all that should remain is the performance you are about to make. Own that version.

The point of this technique is to ensure that you emphatically close the learning process. You should accept that, at that moment, you have done all you can and there is nothing else you can do, and then concentrate on getting yourself into the performance mind-set.

### Travelling to the Lodge

Your journey to the Lodge may be your final chance for rehearsal. Maybe you are a member of a Provincial Lodge and you live nearby, in which case the short journey may be of little or no consequence. However, many Masons live some distance from their Lodges, and the journey is substantial.

We can't cover every possible permutation, so here are some simple decisions that you might consider when travelling to a Lodge meeting where you are going to be delivering a substantial piece of Ritual.

Firstly the journey to the Lodge is perhaps the last and best opportunity to run through the Ceremony, so you may want to avoid hooking up with any of your other Brethren, so you can travel into town alone.

The second decision is usually whether to drive or take public transport. Of course, if you drive you can't drink, so that is a separate consideration. But in terms of your Ritual, driving allows you to recite out-loud, which of course is impossible on the bus or on the train.

For me, I will usually choose the driving option if I'm comfortable that I've mastered the work I'm doing and I just want to practice my delivery.

On the other hand, if I've hit some obstacles along the way, or if I've been asked to do something at short notice, then the journey to the Lodge is the last opportunity for me to work with the Book, in which case public transport is the best option.

### Alcohol

Here's a surprise; Masonry and Drinking are commonly practiced together (well, not at exactly the same time, but definitely on the same day). I'm sure there are Masonic Centres which don't have bars inside or pubs next door, but I haven't come across one yet!

Most Masons I know like a drink with their friends before and/or after the meeting, so it would be disingenuous to insist that you avoid alcohol on a day where you are going to deliver Ritual in the Lodge.

However, I have on occasions, seen defeat snatched from the jaws of victory by a Brother who had one too many before giving his performance. If you are naturally nervous, please avoid the temptation to use drinks before the meeting to relax, because it rarely works.

Often the problem is that Brethren fail to eat properly before the meeting, maybe because they're saving themselves for the Festive Board. This is dangerous, because by the time you stand up in the Lodge to deliver your Ceremony, it may be seven or eight hours since breakfast time, and the effect of those couple of beers you had in the pub before the meeting will be greatly amplified. It will almost definitely impair your intellectual powers, particularly your memory and your powers of recall.

I don't want to be a hypocrite, and I am certainly no advertisement for temperance myself, but as a general rule I would advise no more than one drink in advance of the meeting if you are going to be performing Ritual. There's plenty of time for 'relaxation' once your Work is done!

On the Big Day, why not head straight over to the Temple and squeeze in some rehearsal time before everyone else gets there. Check with the Tyler that it's OK first.

## Prompting

Many Lodges will have their own 'traditions' for Prompting. In some Lodges, there may be a complete ban on Ritual books in the Temple (three cheers!!!), in which case it will probably fall to the IPM or another Senior Officer to be the Prompter from memory.

Irrespective, the most important advice is that you should speak to your nominated Prompter beforehand, and ensure that he has a clear understanding of how you will request prompts. Hopefully you can have this conversation at a Lodge of Instruction meeting, so that your Prompter has the opportunity to observe how you work, the speed of your delivery, the length of your pauses, and so on. The Ritualist and his Prompter are a team. A good Prompter will know exactly how to help you without interfering with your performance.

Why is this understanding important? Well, if you have trained your power of recall discussed earlier, you may sometimes need a slightly longer pause in order to find the next sentence, and you really don't want your Prompter to jump in whilst you are focused on digging deep inside for your words.

## On Arrival

Don't expect that anyone is going to ask you about your Ritual once you arrive at the Lodge. If you need to have any conversations, for example with the DC, other Working Officers, or even the WM, try to get there early and see them in plenty of time, because once the DC starts forming the Procession your chance is gone and everyone will be too busy to speak to you.

Assuming that the Lodge Room or Temple is open and empty whilst the Brethren are dressing for the Meeting, it's a good idea to go in and have a little rehearsal or run through, again just for re-assurance. In many Lodges, the DC will instruct Working Officers, particularly Deacons, to arrive early in order that a rehearsal of the floor work can be held, which is always a smart thing to do. This final run through is the last chance to pick up any little glitches, and for you it is also an ideal opportunity to re-confirm your competence.

If you are performing a Lecture, you should definitely try to 'walk the walk' to get from your seat to your performance position, so that you have a feel for how long it will take.

Next, you should practise the "Line of Commitment" technique you learned. Stand in position, breathe deeply, make a quick checklist of your competence and comfort, then take a short step forwards over your Line of Commitment and begin. It's unlikely that anyone will object if you start to rehearse out loud, even if it's only the first few words.

You should also practice your finish, particularly if it involves a salute to the Chair. When you are finished, for real, the DC or ADC will come and pick you up again and take you back to your seat. So you may need to stand still for a few seconds whilst the DC gets to you. Make sure you know which direction he will approach from, and which direction you should face while you wait. This is really just common sense, but its mastery of these little details that will boost your confidence and underpin your contribution to a seamless meeting.

**Where to Sit**

This is easy if you are in Office. The decision is already made for you.

If you are not in Office, and are being brought up to perform a Lecture, or another element of the Ceremony, you should talk to the DC before the meeting and ask him where he would like you to sit. He or his Assistant will be coming to pick you up in the course of their perambulations, so let the DC decide for you.

If he says he doesn't mind, it's a good idea to position yourself around half way between the DC's position and the point of Delivery, which will vary depending on the Ceremony and whether your Lodge squares. That way the DC can easily find you.

**Beginning and Ending a Lecture**

In some Lodges, it is customary to salute the WM (in the correct Degree of course) at the beginning and end of your rendition. This is a sign of respect, and should be instructed and practiced at Lodge of Instruction, but if you are in any doubt on the day of the meeting, again you should ask the DC before the meeting. Remember to remind yourself which Degree you are in, so you use the right sign.

Once you are placed in your position, you are in complete control of the starting point and the speed of delivery. Remember what we practiced in Chapter 7; don't be tempted to speed up and rush your delivery.

## Final Mental Rehearsal

Almost every Mason I ever met gets nervous before they deliver a Ceremony or a Ritual passage. This is particularly common for Lectures such as Charges and Tracing Boards.

You would be unusual if you didn't have a few butterflies just before you get up; it's a good sign that you are comfortable that you are ready and fully rehearsed.

There's no hard and fast rule about continuing to practise silently during the meeting, because the situation varies enormously. However, since you have already confirmed your competence, it is most unlikely that you will gain any new benefits or make any amazing new discoveries at this late stage. Having passed your 'cut-off point', its fine to think about what you are going to do, but don't try to make any changes. Of course you will naturally think about the task ahead whilst you are waiting your turn, but you should trust yourself that you have the resources you need.

If you are silently rehearsing, and you find you have forgotten something, don't panic. This is common, because there is often some other distraction which is impacting on your focus. The learning process you have completed has solidified and consolidated your Work as a 'whole piece' in your memory. The out-loud rehearsing you did in Stage Three has also imprinted an audio-image, so when you get up to perform, your subconscious should be feeding you the words as a flow. You haven't forgotten anything!

## Be Ready

Make sure you have read the summons, so that you know exactly where you are going to be in the running order. There's nothing worse than being in your bubble in a Lodge Meeting when suddenly your name is called out and it's time for your Work, which you thought was happening later!

If you are being 'inserted' in a Ceremony, for example for Working Tools or a Charge, you should have practiced the sequence with the whole team at LoI. But if you're not sure, make sure you discreetly follow the Ceremony in your book (if it's allowed) so that you're completely prepared when the time comes. You need to maintain your calm as much as possible. You will only stress if you lose the thread.

## Posture and Delivery

We agreed to keep this simple. You should have been able to work out your delivery 'style' in Lodge of Instruction, so there's no reason to change any of it at this stage. Three simple instructions;

- Stand up straight, be natural, and try to relax your body.

- Speak clearly, at a moderate speed. Keep breathing, pause often.

- Try not to wave your hands around too much!!

If you have stuck to the system in this book, you should have gone through the visualisation (or kinaesthetic simulation) of how it is going to be when you step up to begin, so you shouldn't have any shocks or surprises.

Good Luck!

## Chapter 8 Summary

- On Meeting Day, rehearse as many times as you can, starting with your Bathroom Routine.

- Plan your journey to give yourself the right kind of rehearsal or practice time on the way.

- Avoid drinking before the Meeting; save it for later when you have something to celebrate!

- Check in with your Prompter, so you're both on the same page.

- Try to get a 'walk through' in the Temple, before the meeting.

- Sit in the right place, stay relaxed, and be mentally and physically ready.

- When your turn comes, stand up straight and take a breath to relax

- Focus your resources and step over your Line of Commitment

# 9
# THE NEXT STEPS

## The Day After

So, you did it! You taught yourself a Ceremony and you delivered it in the Lodge. I'm guessing that it went OK for you?

## How Do You Feel?

Maybe you just feel relieved that it's over and done with, or maybe you really enjoyed the sense of achievement, because you really did something special. Hopefully you didn't hate every minute of the process, and now you understand that a systematic approach can deliver a strong performance you'll be ready for the next one.

Once the Festive Board is over and you've been congratulated on a job well done, there's a new set of processes for you to follow in order to take the best from the whole experience and apply it for the future.

When you go to bed on the night of the meeting things may be different for you. For the last few weeks, every night has involved a systematic rehearsal of your Ritual, but tonight you're in the clear, right?

Wrong!

Being a participant in the Ritual in your Lodge involves you building a library of Ceremonies in your memory, because it's a fair bet that you'll be called upon to do each one more than once. If your first encounter with the Work was as Junior Deacon, for example, you'll probably have another chance to perform the same Degree work again, either during the remainder of your year in the SD office, or as a stand-in at some future date, or even in another Lodge if you should expand your Masonry beyond your Mother Lodge in the future.

## So What Did You Learn?

In the immediate aftermath of a 'performance' it's a good idea to review what happened. I'd be surprised if you are entirely happy with your performance. Maybe the things you expected to trip you up were actually fine, but you struggled with something unexpected? Maybe you thought (no, maybe you *knew*) that you'd followed the system and you'd thoroughly learned your words, but you still got stuck a couple of times and needed prompts?

Listen, don't worry about it. Unless it was a complete disaster, in which case let's go back a few steps and try it again, you have accomplished your first mission, and from here you can only improve.

## Protecting Your Assets

You just spent several weeks learning a tricky passage or Ceremony, and the natural temptation is to say 'Phew' and forget about it for now.

However, now is the right time to cement this work into your memory, so that it will be there more easily the next time you need it. By spending just a little more time on this Ritual now, you could save yourself many hours of re-learning in the future.

The pressure is off you. Hopefully nobody is expecting you to do this work again in the short term. If you enjoyed yourself this time, you'll probably want to take on something new and more challenging for your next outing. Maybe the natural progression is that you will do the next Degree at the next Meeting. Whatever the case, it's a good time to protect what you just learned and delivered.

I recommend that for the next week or so, you find time to recite the Work you just learned, at least once a day. Without the performance pressure you'll be much more relaxed about it, and it will thoroughly cement itself into your long-term memory.

Simply put; until you get some new work to do, keep practising the old work.

## Straight After the Meeting

The time to start is when you go to bed on the night of the meeting, when the performance itself is still fresh in your short-term memory. This gives you a golden opportunity to review it. Lie down in the dark, close your eyes, and replay the actual performance in your mind. You may be surprised to find that any mistakes or prompts will magically reappear, and you'll have a chance to analyse each one and add those analyses to the bank of information you already stored about this Ceremony whilst you were learning it.

I know; it's the last thing you feel like doing right now, but I promise you that it will pay huge dividends down the line.

## Acknowledge Your Strengths and Weaknesses

If you followed the method in this book so far, you'll know that the central core of this Ritual method is systematic organisation. In keeping with that, here are some key metrics you can check against your performance. If you're serious about improving for the next time (maybe you don't need to!) then you can score yourself against each criterion;

- Did you actually forget any of the passage(s)?

- Did you need prompts to get from one section to the next?

- Did you feel confident in the delivery?

- Do you think you were you boring?

- Did you need to ad-lib any of the words or phrases (this can actually be a positive)?

- Do you feel you appeared to be physically relaxed during the performance?

Try this as an exercise, just for your own information. The outcome will enable you ascertain where you need to focus your additional work, or allocate more time in the future.

It's quite common for Lodge of Instruction to hold a little Post-Mortem at some point following a meeting. You should try to attend, because this is probably the only time you can expect to get something like an honest critique of your Work.

### Filling the Gap In Your Life!

For many people, the next day after the meeting is a bit of an anti-climax. Because you spent the last few weeks working to a disciplined schedule, now that the pressure is off, you'll find gaps in your life with nothing to fill them.

Having established that you can follow the System, and fit learning around and inside your normal daily routine, it's important not to lose the structure. You've re-organised your life to accommodate Ritual Learning, so why would you want to go back to the old way of doing things?

If you are in a Working Office, such as Deacon, or maybe

even WM, it's quite simple. You should already know what the Work is going to be at the next meeting, and what your part is going to entail, and if you don't, a quick e-mail or SMS to the Lodge Secretary will soon provide the answer. So you can go straight to the Book and start working on your next Ceremony. Hopefully there is enough time for you to set up the process as we did before.

Alternately, if you were delivering Tools, Charges or Lectures, it's really important not to wait until the next Standing Committee or Lodge of Instruction to get your assignment, because if that's a few days or weeks away, you'll be losing time and slipping out of the system you learned. So be smart; even if you don't know what precise Work might be available to you at the next meeting, you should know what Ceremony is planned. So pick the most appropriate Work, again which might be the Tools, or the Charge, and start on it straight away. As we explained earlier, if you're an active attendee at Standing Committee or LoI, you can usually manoeuvre yourself into the position of being invited to do the work you want, at least some of the time.

Most Lodges have a long Summer Break, and this is can be both a problem and an opportunity. If you are in a Working Office, a five-or-six-month break can mean you get very rusty at the basics, like opening and closing the Lodge. It's important to practice these 'standards' every week or two during the Summer.

If you are not in Office, and you haven't been allocated any specific work (chances are there isn't a Standing Committee or LoI meeting coming up until September), this is a great opportunity for you to take on something like the First or Second Tracing Board, which you can easily do on your own. Imagine being able to offer that to your Lodge when the year starts again.

Your Masonic career is long, so no Ritual will ever be

wasted.

When it comes to the Lectures, consult the recommended timetable of each of the major Ceremonies, which is shown in Appendix A.

This time you are smarter than you were the first time. You will have figured out the techniques that worked really well for you. For example, do you need to allow more time for the first stage, the 'cramming' of the work? Or maybe that was fine but it took longer than you thought to iron out the kinks in Stage 2. Whatever the case, you are the best person to judge your own capabilities. You can use whichever of the techniques worked for you, and indeed add to them if you found methods or variations that worked better.

But you must stick to the Three-Stage Approach: Cramming, Polishing and Rehearsing.

Remember; C.P.R.

## Re-Learning and Revising

Once you've gone through the pain of learning something once, and delivered it, the second time is a lot easier, because if you learned it well enough to deliver it competently, then you have successfully implanted it into your subconscious memory. It has become a part of you. So dragging it back to the surface a second time is going to be a lot easier than learning it all over again, and the third time will be easier still.

The first time I was required to perform a Raising Ceremony from the Chair was during my Masters Year in my Mother Lodge. Using most of the methods previously explained, and with the benefit of a Lodge of Instruction which, for around two months, just about dedicated itself to this Ceremony, it took me around four months to get it to the point where I was able to deliver it. I won't say that it was flawless; far from it. I am sure I made a lot of mistakes, most of which I managed to cover without anyone noticing, and I probably took a few prompts as well. But it went OK, we didn't kill or even injure the candidate, and we had a nice drink afterwards.

The next time I did the Ceremony was a few years later, and it took me a month and two LoI's to get it done. The performance was infinitely better than the first time, though still far from perfect.

Since then I have grabbed the opportunity to do the Third Degree maybe six or seven times in my Mother Lodge, and these days it takes around a fortnight of revision and one complete run through at LoI and it's done. It's still not perfect, I still miss a sentence out here and there, and occasionally I'll need a prompt (because I'm getting a bit older now), but these days I only need the Book, or rather the transcript on my Smartphone, to get it done.

It's my favourite Craft Ceremony. Whenever there is a Third Degree imminent, I make sure that I have revised it just in case. Because you never know what might happen or when you might have to step up at the last minute and fill in for the WM whose car wouldn't start!

These days, Grand Lodge encourages the 'splitting up' of the larger Ceremonies, such as the Raising, so that more Brethren can be involved, and this is a great strategy for Lodges. Continuing with the Third Degree Ceremony, here are some ways that can be shared around;

If practical the WM should always perform the first half of the Ceremony in its entirety, right through to the point where the Candidate has been 'raised' and retires to restore his personal comforts. Many Lodges call-off during this break in the Ceremony.

It is also common to change the occupant of the WM's chair for the second half of the Ceremony (nominally referred to as the Traditional History). This second part contains several distinct opportunities for other Brethren to take part;

- Explanation of the Third Tracing Board; this varies in length depending on the Workings, but it's quite short and much easier to learn than either the First or Second Tracing Boards. The Logic Ritual version is particularly engaging

- The Working Tools

- The Charge after Raising; this is often missed out because of 'time issues'. Which is bizarre because it normally takes less than two minutes to deliver, and is a sublime and exquisite passage

I try to maintain the Raising Ceremony in a current condition all the time, so that I am able to step in and take on any individual part of it if needed, even at short notice. This is good for me, because it provides a regular opportunity to work in the Lodge, and it's good for the Lodge, because it gives us options. You might consider something similar yourself in the future.

## Conclusion

If you are serious about Ritual, either because you are working your way through the Offices in order to eventually take the Chair of your Lodge, or alternately if you are simply interested in participating in the Lodge by delivering Charges and Tracing Boards, there is no reason why you should ever be in a position where you are not learning or preparing the next piece of work.

If you adopt this philosophy, you will always have something to occupy you in a quiet moment. And you will always have a way of getting to sleep at night!

# TAILPIECE

I hope that this book has helped you to discover a passion for Ritual, or at very least given you what you need in order to 'have a go'.

If your experience was positive, please take a few moments to Review the book on Amazon.

If you have any comments or suggestions, or would simply like to exchange opinions on any aspect of Masonic Ritual, please join the Forum on

www.learningmasonicritual.com

There's also a Facebook Page called 'Learning Masonic Ritual' which is checked every day, so if you have urgent questions on any kind of Ritual, please post there and I'll endeavour to help, or connect you with someone that can.

I'm always interested in hearing about tips and tricks which improve the learning and delivery of good Ritual, so if you have something to share, please bring it, and I'll try to include it in the next update of this book.

Sincerely and Fraternally

Rick Smith

rs@learningmasonicritual.com

| Recommended Timetable for Lectures (Days) | | | | |
|---|---|---|---|---|
| Ceremony | C | P | R | Total |
| 1$^{st}$ Working Tools | 6 | 3 | 3 | 12 |
| Charge to Initiate | 30 | 15 | 15 | 60 |
| 1$^{st}$ Tracing Board (Standard) | 40 | 20 | 20 | 80 |
| 1$^{st}$ Tracing Board (Extended) | 60 | 30 | 30 | 120 |
| 2$^{nd}$ Working Tools | 14 | 7 | 7 | 28 |
| 2$^{nd}$ Charge After Passing | 14 | 7 | 7 | 28 |
| 2$^{nd}$ Tracing Board (Standard) | 40 | 20 | 20 | 80 |
| 2$^{nd}$ Tracing Board (Extended) | 60 | 30 | 30 | 120 |
| 3$^{rd}$ Charge After Raising | 10 | 5 | 5 | 20 |
| 3rd Tracing Board (Logic) | 10 | 5 | 5 | 20 |
| Long Closing (Taylors) | 14 | 7 | 7 | 28 |
| Grand Lodge Cert (Taylors) | 20 | 10 | 10 | 40 |
| Grand Lodge Cert (Emulation) | 30 | 15 | 15 | 60 |

# Now Available on Amazon for Kindle

21099095R00081

Printed in Poland
by Amazon Fulfillment
Poland Sp. z o.o., Wrocław